C000052971

Patricia
Ernie W

Pythons

Everything about Selection, Care,
Nutrition, Diseases, Breeding,
and Behavior

With 60 Color Photographs

Illustrations by David Wenzel

BARRON'S

Dedication

This book is dedicated to my husband, Dick, in appreciation of many hours in the field.

Patti Bartlett

This book is dedicated to my wife Darcie Richardson, without whose help and enthusiasm I would still be behind a desk at Woodland Park Zoo, shoveling stacks of paper. It is also dedicated to Dr. Bernard Bechtel of Valdosta, Georgia. Dr. Bechtel was one of the first people to understand the genetics of colors and pigmentation in snakes, and our hobby owes him a great deal of thanks.

Ernie Wagner

All inquiries should be addressed to:
Barron's Educational Series, Inc.
250 Wireless Boulevard
Hauppauge, NY 11788

ISBN-13: 978-0-8120-9365-0
ISBN-10: 0-8120-9365-8

Library of Congress Catalog Card No. 97-38570

Library of Congress Cataloging-in-Publication Data
Bartlett, Patricia Pope, 1949–
    Pythons : everything about selection, care, nutrition, diseases, breeding, and behavior / Patricia Bartlett and Ernie Wagner.
        p.   cm.
    Includes bibliographical references and index.
    ISBN 0-8120-9365-8
    1. Pythons as pets. I. Wagner, Ernie. II. Title.
SF459.S5B359   1997
639.3'96—dc21
                            97-38570
                              CIP

Printed in China

19 18 17 16 15 14 13 12

About the Authors

Patricia Bartlett is an historian/naturalist who has worked in museums for 15 years. She began her career with reptiles by working for Ross Allen, a Florida herpetologist who first opened Silver Springs, a fresh-water spring resort where the early Tarzan movies were filmed. She has worked as an editor, writer, museum director, and data analyst, has observed reptiles and amphibians in the field for 30 years, and has written or coauthored 11 books on their captive care.

Ernie Wagner worked for Woodland Park Zoo in Seattle for 25 years, starting as a pony leader and ending up as Curator of Reptiles. Along the way he acquired a great deal of experience with birds and mammals, but especially with reptiles. He has given a wide variety of lectures on reptile behavior and published over two dozen papers on various aspects of breeding and husbandry. For the past 15 years he has owned and operated Poikilotherm Farms, a private reptile breeding facility. He is currently a columnist for *Reptiles* magazine, writing on a monthly basis about the care and breeding of reptiles.

Photo Credits

Zig Leszczynski: pages 9, 12, 13, 25, 29 top, 48 top and bottom, 72, 84, 90; Bob Guerriere: pages 17, 20, 21 top and bottom, 44 top and bottom, 45 top and bottom, 52; Bill Love: page 16; Ernie Wagner: pages 8, 32; all other photos by Patricia and R. D. Bartlett.

Photos on the Covers

Front cover: diamond-carpet python intergrade, *Morelia spilota* ssp.; inside front cover: adult green tree python, *Morelia viridis;* inside back cover: hatchling green tree python, *Morelia viridis;* back cover: spotted python, *Antaresia maculosa.*

Important Note

The subject of this book is the keeping and care of nonpoisonous snakes. Snake keepers should realize, however, that even the bite of a snake regarded as nonpoisonous can have harmful consequences. So see a doctor immediately after any snake bite.

Handling giant serpents requires a lot of experience and a great sense of responsibility. Carelessness can be deadly! Inexperienced snake keepers and snake keepers who have small children are therefore urgently advised not to keep giant serpents.

Electrical appliances used in the care of snakes must carry a valid "UL approved" marking. Everyone using such equipment should be aware of the dangers involved with it. It is strongly recommended that you purchase a device that will instantly shut off the electrical current in the event of failure in the appliances or wiring. A circuit-protection device with a similar function has to be installed by a licensed electrician.

Contents

Acknowledgments

We would like to acknowledge the python breeders, whose expertise and generosity have made this book possible.

Thirty years ago, nobody bred pythons, and the lack of knowledge was dismissed with "there are plenty of them out there—who needs to breed them?" For some species, changing and diminishing habitat and vastly increased legislation have decreased the number imported. For other species, like the ball pythons, the numbers imported have increased, even more reason to develop fail-safe husbandry techniques.

But farsighted individuals, such as Eugene Bessette, Tracy and David Barker, Stan Chiras, John Meltzer, Regis Opferman, and Trooper Walsh looked ahead and made plans to propagate these fascinating snakes. And they've shared their knowledge with others, increasing interest in the snakes as a whole and in pythons in particular. They deserve our thanks and our support in their endeavors.

The bright coloration of the jungle carpet python assures that this snake will long be a hobbyist's favorite.

The strongly contrasting normal color phase of the Burmese python makes this snake easy to recognize in the pet market.

Understanding Pythons

Pythons are relatively primitive snakes belonging to the subfamily Pythoninae within the family Boidae. Boidae, in turn, is one of 11 families in the suborder Serpentes, the snakes.

Binomial Nomenclature

Our system of classification, designed by Carl von Linne in 1756, uses physical similarities to group animals or plants by ever-more rigid criteria. Snakes are grouped together, and as the criteria gets more selective, snakes of similar appearances and habits are grouped together.

Within the subfamily of pythons, arboreal pythons with heat-sensing pits along their lips (green tree pythons) are grouped separately from terrestrial pythons that have heavy bodies and short tails (blood pythons). Each different type of snake eventually

White-lipped Python

Blood Python

Pythons show a wide diversity within the subfamily, from size to weight to habitat. Here, the contrast between the length and bulk of the white-lipped and blood pythons is shown.

ends up with two names, one for the genus and one for the species. When isolated populations exist that are still identifiable as the same type of snake, a third name, the trinomial, is added.

The term *primitive* indicates that these snakes were some of the first snakes to evolve. Primitive snakes display features that link them to lizards. These features include a rudimentary pelvic girdle in the form of cloacal spurs, and lungs of equal sizes. Advanced snakes, like the rat snakes and whip snakes, have only one functional lung and no cloacal spurs.

Pythons are divided into about 26 species, depending on which authority you accept. (Like other fields, different researchers are most emphatic that their own criteria represent the best way to define the species.) If past trends are any indication, new divisions and redefinitions will be issued, compared, and criticized. They may even be accepted.

Python Characteristics

Pythons range in size from very big (the Burmese and reticulated pythons, with the potential of over 20 feet [6 m] and over 200 pounds [91 kg]), to small (the Children's pythons don't get much bigger than 24 inches [61 cm] in length). No matter what the size, they are all constrictors. Some burrow-hunting species have developed novel ways of using their coils to catch prey within the confines of a burrow, but they are still constrictors nonetheless.

Most pythons are nocturnal hunters and some species have heat sensory pits along the edges of their lips to aid in finding warm-blooded prey.

Kingdom		Animalia (all animals, from amoebas to humans)
Phylum		Chordata (animals with notocords, a form of spinal cord)
	Subphylum	Vertebrata (animals with backbones)
Class		Reptilia (all reptiles)
Order		Squamata (possessing scales, the snakes and lizards)
	Suborder	Serpentes (all snakes, some 3000 kinds)
Family		Boidae (divided into two groups, boas and pythons)
	Subfamily	Pythoninae (only pythons)
Genus		Morelia (one of 11 genera within the subfamily)
Species		viridis (one of the six species within the genus)

Pythons versus Boas

Pythons are distinct from boas in their reproduction. Most boas retain the eggs inside the body until they hatch; pythons lay eggs. Boas are termed ovoviviparous: the eggs inside the females are surrounded by a membrane instead of a hard shell. When the babies are ready to be born, the eggs are dispelled one at a time, the babies break through the membrane, and the young crawl away.

Pythons are oviparous: the eggs are surrounded by a thin, parchmentlike shell. Females of most species of pythons will coil around their eggs and stay with them during the incubation period. Some species are actually able to generate heat through continuous body contractions (thermoregulation) and so help the incubation process by raising their own temperature, and consequently, the temperature of the eggs. When the babies hatch, they cut a slit through the egg shell with an egg tooth on the tip of their nose and crawl out.

Python eggs take about two months to hatch and the eggs seem to have more specific temperature requirements than other snake eggs. If python eggs are incubated at inadequate temperatures, large numbers of stillbirths and birth defects such as spinal kyphosis (backward curvature of the spine) or incomplete develop-

ment will result. Oddly enough, when the incubation temperature is too low, you will also frequently see anomalies in the pattern, such as striping. Be aware that if you're offered an unusual striped specimen, the pattern may be the result of incubation temperatures and not genetics.

Python Life Span

Like most snakes, the python life span averages 20 to 25 years, but a snake kept under good conditions may live a lot longer—a ball python in the Highland Park Zoo (Pennsylvania) lived for 47 years! An explanation once offered when a captive python inexplicably died—"Well, we don't know how old it was when we caught it"—seems hauntingly inadequate in retrospect.

The cloacal spurs are used during breeding to initiate the breeding response in the female.

Both normal-colored and albino babies are hatching from this clutch of Burmese python (Python molurus bivittatus) *eggs. Clutch size varies from 15 to 60 eggs.*

Habitat

Pythons were once thought to be essentially an Old World snake. One "almost-a-python" species, the New World python, has recently been reclassified out of the boa subfamily and tucked into its own family, Loxoceminae. (Since it is an egg-laying species, it is termed a python for now. Next year it may be classified another way.) Except for this single North American species, pythons are found literally on the other side of the globe, in tropical parts of Africa, Asia, and Australia. Within these warm zones, pythons are found in a wide variety of environments, from very humid and wet to very dry. Although pythons have found ways to survive in very hot climates (nocturnal activity is one of them), their geographic limitations are proscribed by low temperatures.

With the exception of one or two relatively small arboreal species, most pythons are primarily ground-dwellers, living in burrows or under some kind of ground shelter, occasionally basking in the daytime but doing most of their hunting at night. During extremely hot and dry conditions, some species will go underground and become inactive until conditions change. With most, the climatic change that triggers reproduction is the onset of cooler temperatures.

Endangered Status

Many species of pythons are endangered in their native countries. The loss of habitat is the main reason. (Habitat destruction is also a serious threat to the long-term survival of many nonreptilian species.)

The skin trade and hunting for food (in some cultures, protein is wherever

The variably speckled Loxocemus bicolor *is the only New World species of python.*

you can find it) have also taken their toll. The pet trade consumes large numbers of one or two species, such as the African ball python. Gravid females are selectively taken from the wild and maintained in captivity in their country of origin. Once the females have laid their eggs, the females are exported to the pet trade, the eggs are hatched, and those babies are also exported. Legally imported counts for 1994 were in excess of 40,000, and slightly higher in 1995. It's hard to comprehend how any snake population can withstand this sort of reduction without serious long-term effects.

While the numbers of pythons that are legally imported are monitored by CITES, the Convention in Trade Endangered Species, the care of these animals is not. Conditions under which the animals are held and eventually shipped often leads to disease and death. Wholesalers are dealing in numbers, not in captive care techniques.

Acquiring Your Python

Snakes are ideal pets in many ways. They are quiet, easy to care for, and can be left for a week's vacation with a "sitter." But there are some special considerations when choosing to live with a python.

Before You Buy a Python

You'll be together for a long time. Remember, this is a long-lived pet, certainly up to 20 years or more, far longer than a cat or a dog.

Size

These are constricting snakes, snakes that tightly hold the prey in their coils until the animal suffocates. Depending on the species, your python can certainly grow to 16 feet (5 m) and weigh more than most grown men. A snake of that size is a strong snake. Not everyone wants to house, feed, or care for pythons of this

Pythons more than eight feet (2.4 meters) long need two people for safe handling.

size, and the most important consideration is that *one* person cannot safely handle a python larger than 10 feet (3 m). This is the primary risk factor involved in keeping large snakes, such as the Burmese; they are often deceptively gentle, and that's the problem. You tend to forget that this creature is a capable predator, and the instinctive predator behavior can be provoked by fear or by something as seemingly innocuous as the lingering scent on your arm of your pet bird.

Food

Snakes are guided by instinct, and one of those instincts tells a snake that when it smells food and something in the area is moving, the moving object is prey. A big snake is a strong snake. People have actually been killed by their large pet pythons by making mistakes at feeding time. Having said that, we need to remind you that thousands of large pythons are kept as pets all over the country, and in the last ten years there have been only about half a dozen documented python-related deaths.

In addition to adult size, another consideration is type of food. Rabbits will probably be the meal of choice for large pythons but do you want to offer these gentle, doe-eyed creatures to your snake? You *can* obtain frozen rabbits, thaw them in warm water, and then feed them to your snake, but the process is time-consuming. Many people find the prospect of storing frozen rabbits among the frozen peas depressing, and the aspect of buying and killing live rabbits no better.

There are, however, several species of attractive, good-natured pythons that get no larger than gopher or pine snakes and that will happily eat prekilled mice. We state "prekilled" because feeding live mice (or rats) to your python is asking for trouble. When a rodent is confined with a snake, if the snake doesn't immediately kill and eat the rodent, the rodent may harm the snake. Every veterinarian has dealt with a snake that has a gnawed-off tail tip, pierced eye, or partially eaten vertebral column, and hear from the owner, "I didn't know a mouse would hurt my snake!"

Even if you put aside all humanitarian feelings for mice or rats and take a purely practical stance, keeping food for your pythons on hand is easier if the food items can be stored in your freezer. If your freezer space is limited, frozen mice take up less room than frozen rabbits. If you have no room in your freezer whatever for any sort of snake food, commercially made canned "snake sausages" are available. Be advised, however, that these canned items are fairly new to the market, and their long-term effect on pythons has not yet been determined.

Temperament

This is another important consideration. Are you interested in a pet that is gentle and easy to handle, or are you more interested in a colorful snake that may be bad-tempered, but makes a beautiful or impressive display? Children's, blotched, Stimson's, or ball pythons are easygoing, small-sized pythons that generally do well in captivity (of course there are caveats; see the species accounts for these). Green tree, reticulated, and Burmese pythons do make impressive display animals (again, please see the species accounts for the think-twice caveats). Burmese pythons are known

Pythons vary widely in adult size and in temperament.

for their gentle dispositions, but reticulated pythons are not.

Bites

Every hobbyist has a favorite story about being bitten. Generally, any conversation that deals with being bitten is punctuated with high hilarity, because we all understand that could have been us ("There I was, my nose bitten and both of my thumbs in the snake's mouth, and all Fred wanted to do was get the camera!"). Before you join this not very elite group, you may want to know why a python bite hurts so much, and how a snake can draw so much blood. Bites can be serious business.

The essential explanation is that pythons have anywhere from 100 to 150 teeth, and the teeth in the front are longer than the teeth in the back. As far as food is concerned, when a snake's survival depends on its ability to snag and hold onto prey items using only its teeth and coils, the longer teeth in the front mean a real advantage.

Ball pythons (Python regius) *are commonly small, good-natured, readily available, and comparatively inexpensive.*

But pythons don't always want to devour what they bite. Sometimes the bite is out of fear, or is an indication of territorial aggression. A fearful python tends to bite and then loosely hold on. Any motion on your part simply pulls the teeth through the wound. The wound size is largely determined by the size of the teeth. The larger the python, the bigger the teeth; for a 12-footer (3.7 m), you're dealing with teeth a half-inch (1 cm) long. A fear-inspired bite can mean a visit to the emergency room of your local hospital, stitches, shots, and a lot of attention you'd rather not have.

If you are bitten by your hatchling or small adult python, wash the affected area and apply a light compress to stop the bleeding. If any of the snake's teeth are left in the wound, remove them. Keep the area dry and clean until the cuts are completely closed. If you're bitten by a python larger than 6 ft. (1.8 m), seek medical attention.

Legal Considerations

Legal considerations need to be a factor when choosing a pet python.

Many states and local municipalities have laws restricting the keeping of snakes over a certain size. If you are purchasing your snake from a local pet shop, the shop employees should—*should*—be able to tell you about local size restrictions, however, keep in mind that most pet shops will not take back a snake or refund the purchase price, no matter what your reason for the return.

If you find a breeder or dealer from out of state and decide to have your python shipped to you, be aware that U.S. Fish and Wildlife restricts the interstate shipment of the Indian python (*Python molurus molurus*) without a federal permit. All other pythons can be shipped from state to state without federal permits.

All pythons are CITES animals, which means that the importer must apply for and receive a CITES permit before the snake can be imported for commercial purposes. Depending on the kind of python, additional permits may be required. Once the python is within the United States, no federal or state permits are needed for commerce, shipment, or ownership.

To obtain more specific information on size, temperament, and captive requirements of the types of pythons you are considering buying, refer to the species accounts beginning on page 56. To check the legalities of specific species, call your municipal government, your state game commission, and the Department of the Interior.

Other Considerations

We also strongly urge the purchase of captive-bred, captive-hatched (cb/ch) pythons over wild-caught animals. In addition to the decreased pressure on wild populations, there are some very real and economic reasons for this choice:

1. Captive-bred animals will usually be free of parasites and less stressed than wild-caught animals. They are more accustomed to easily obtained food; ball pythons from the wild, for instance, are notoriously picky feeders, wanting, perhaps, only what they fed on in the wild, or maybe black gerbils, or only white-footed mice, or only road-killed squirrels, or maybe just deciding what they ate last time isn't going to be what they want this time. In contrast, a captive-born baby ball python will present none of these feeding problems.

2. Many pet stores offer only cb/ch pythons, and for some species that are protected in their country of origin, this is the only way they are available.

If your local pet store does not have the kind of python you are looking for, try your local herpetological society or talk to other reptile keepers about sources. There are also several very good national reptile magazines available at newsstands; check the display and classified ad sections of these magazines.

Buying Your Snake

If you buy your snake from a local source, handle the snake yourself before you buy it. Look for any problems such as wheezing, body lumps, parasites, or contusions. Find out what the snake has been eating, and how recently it has fed.

Buying from a dealer is a little more complex, but not overwhelmingly so. Dealers mail out lists of their animals, usually on a monthly basis. Sometimes you can call and ask for a sample price list, or ask about subscription prices. There's a modest charge for an annual subscription, about $10.

When the list arrives, all you need to do is to spend a few minutes reading the section on pythons. Check the sex of the snake(s) (1.2.5 indicates one male, two females, and five yet-to-be sexed snakes), the size, and

Ontogenetic (age related) color changes in the difficult-to-handle green tree python are interesting and dramatic.

any special notes ("the prettiest we've EVER seen!" is a typical, oft-repeated comment).

If you find a python of the species, size, sex, color morph, and price you like, call the dealer and let him or her know you're interested in that particular snake. Ask if it is feeding, and what it feeds on, and talk about the price, payment method, and shipping arrangements.

Price

The price is rarely negotiable unless you're very good friends with the dealer, or unless there's something very wrong with the snake. A dealer doesn't want to sell you a sick snake, but maybe the snake you want is missing its tail tip or is scarred from a recent encounter with another python. Maybe the dealer thinks that python is gravid, a reason for extra caution in shipping and an increase in price.

Payment modes. Reptile dealers deal in cash or in credit cards. A money order, cashier's check, or wire transfer of funds is the same as cash for most dealers. If a dealer will accept

13

your personal check, expect a week or so delay while the check clears the bank. The dealer isn't being petty; you may be ordering a $300 snake, and the dealer may be across the country from you. If you have one of the credit cards the dealer accepts, buying whatever snake you want is faster and even easier than writing a check.

Shipping by Air

Most dealers ship one or two days a week, and they avoid shipping on Fridays when air freight offices may be closed for the weekend. Keep in mind that the air freight charges will be added to the price of the snake, so that $300 python will cost you a minimum of $350.

Give the supplier your full name, address, and phone numbers where you can be reached day and night. Tell the dealer which airport you'll be using (some cities have two airports, and finding out your snake has been shipped to the other airport is at the least frustrating). Try to keep your shipment with the same airline for the entire trip; for live animals, you pay for each airline involved. If you want someone to bring the snake to your door, let the dealer know the name of the door-to-door delivery company you'd like to use.

If size permits, pythons are usually shipped in muslin bags in a styrofoam crate within a wooden crate.

Get the airbill number from the dealer and keep it with you. Find out what day your animals will be shipped to you, and approximately what time they'll arrive—if the shipment isn't delayed because the mail took up all the available room in the plane's cargo bin. The U.S. mail does have priority over freight shipments for the limited room available in the belly bins of planes. You can buy priority service from the freight office, but it will cost you more than the usual "space available" service.

Expect your shipment to take about 24 hours from the time your dealer ships it to you to the time it arrives at your local airport. If the airline hasn't called you by then, call the local airfreight office and ask them for the status of the shipment. They will need your airbill number, which is why you must keep it close at hand for 24 hours before the expected delivery. The airbill number is used to trace the shipment through the airline's computer.

When the shipment arrives check the hours of the freight office so that you can pick up your shipment as soon as possible, especially if the weather is especially cold or especially hot. Although the shipping package will be clearly marked "Do Not Subject to Extremes of Temperature," this won't protect your snakes from accidents.

You'll have to pay any due shipping charges before the shipment will be turned over to you. Once all the financial details are taken care of, open and inspect your shipment at the freight office (just glance inside the bags; no one wants you to take the snake out of the bag at the freight office!).

Reliable dealers guarantee live delivery. If there is a discrepancy, both the dealer and the airline will want you to fill out a claim report on the spot. The report needs to be signed and dated by the airfreight personnel, and you'll need to contact the dealer immediately about the problem.

Bringing Your Python Home

Behavior Notes

Although many pythons will allow gentle handling, go slowly. When you open the bag, reach in and grasp your snake. Do it gently and slowly. Inspect the snake for obvious problems such as ticks, mites, or physical damage. Place the snake in its cage, close the cage, and leave it alone for a few hours. Give the snake time to adjust to the new smells, lighting, and temperature of its cage.

When you open the cage, don't yank the door open and grab for the snake. Move slowly and deliberately. There is only one way for your snake to protest, and that's with its mouth.

Some snakes will never adjust to being handled and will protest these overtures on your part. These pythons include the Macklot's and white-lipped pythons, and the African rock python. They may need to be considered display animals only, and while their size permits (the rock pythons get big), moved and manipulated on a snake hook. If the cage has a hide box with a secure bottom, the hide box with the snake within can be moved for cage cleaning.

Even some species like the burrowing pythons resent being suddenly grasped. Move deliberately and slowly. Do not tap on the cage front. If the snake protests at being handled, use a snake hook to move it to a secure holding area while you clean the cage.

There are two reasons why you do not want the snake to bite you, and these are both for the snake's health. If you jerk your hand away when you get bitten, you'll probably jerk out some of the snake's teeth. Losing

teeth this way makes your snake vulnerable to mouth rot (see page 39), an infection that may become established when there are open wounds in the snake's mouth.

Secondly, if a snake bites you and you overreact and drop the snake, severe and largely undetectable abdominal and vertebral damage can result. Many python species never leave ground level, and are completely incapable of falling without incurring damage.

Captive-Bred Young

Not all pythons must be caught in the wild and imported in order to reach your local pet dealer. Many cb/ch python species, including the endangered ones, are available from captive breeders. It's obvious that a cb/ch animal is more accustomed to captivity than its wild-caught counterpart. Captive-born animals are also accustomed to the foods offered by their keepers. Legalities aside, an olive python that has been feeding on wallabies in the wild may not find even the fluffiest rabbit appetizing, and scenting the unfamiliar food item with the python's preferred prey is going to be difficult.

Consider the Source

The source of your potential pet python and the characteristics of the species should both be considered in deciding what python you want. Research the qualities of the pythons that appeal to you, including their temperament. Some python species are calm, docile creatures that seem to recognize their keeper. Other species never get out of the habit of striking at any human, or even worse, can be calm and collected one moment and then lunge for you the next. Different geographic populations of the same species of python may be calmer and easier to feed, or may mature

Reptile shows are an excellent source of pythons and everything needed to keep them healthy. This is the Florida International Reptile Show, which runs for two days each September in Tampa.

at different sizes. New information about python behavior is made available on a regular basis through monthly publications, scientific journals, in newsletters published by reptile clubs, and on computer reptile chat lines. Both you and your python will benefit from your information gathering *before* (and after) you purchase your snake.

Caging

What kind of caging you can provide in terms of space and materials plays an important role in the selection of your pet python and how well your python will do in captivity.

Cage materials can range from simple, using an aquarium tank as a terrarium, to homemade, creating basically a glass-fronted box, to commercial units, made from fiberglass or mica laminate.

What to Provide

You'll need to provide enough space for the snake, a hiding area, a water bowl, and a heating/lighting source that will heat a basking area to about 90 to 93°F (33–34°C). Arboreal species will need climbing limbs.

Size of Cage

While you're thinking about possible materials, think about space, of the cage itself and how much room you can devote to a cage. As far as the snake is concerned, overall length of the cage should be roughly two-thirds the snake's length; cage width can be a little less, perhaps half the length of your snake. There is room for adjustment in these figures; the goal is to give the snake enough room to turn around easily.

Don't forget that some pythons get big, very big. As your snake matures, the cage size needs to increase as well. A Children's or sawu python, which matures at 3 feet (91 cm), needs a cage at least 24 inches long (61 cm) by 12 inches (30 cm) deep, or the standard 20-gallon (76 L) aquarium size. An adult snake as large as a Burmese will require a room-sized enclosure.

Local and State Regulations

Most states have a minimum cage size, based on the length of the snake. In Florida, for instance, the perimeter measurement of the cage must at least equal the length of the snake.

Types of Caging

Plastic Sweater Boxes

Plastic sweater boxes, with ventilation holes drilled or melted through the sides, are good for many species of smaller pythons. The smaller, shoe-box-sized boxes can come in very

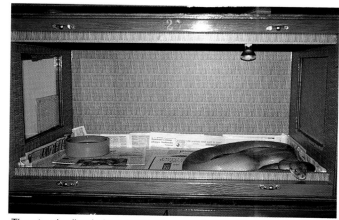

The standardized glass-fronted box can be modified for almost every species of python.

handy if you suddenly hatch a clutch of eggs and have anywhere from 6 to 40 babies to deal with. When the babies are housed one to a box, you can monitor each baby's growth and feeding response. Choose clear plastic boxes over the translucent ones—those made of translucent plastic make observing your pets impossible.

You can fit many of these plastic boxes in a small amount of space, especially if you use a rack. A shoebox rack is very easy to build; it is essentially a bank of shelves with a heat tape set either in the front or along the back edge of the shelves. The heat tape is an economical and efficient way to provide a warmth gradient for each shoebox.

A shoebox rack may mean you can forego the lids to the boxes. Some people have avoided having to drill/melt ventilation holes by eliminating the shoebox lid and leaving ¼-inch (6 mm) of space between the open box and the shelf above it. This allows good ventilation without allowing your snake

A vertical cage provides climbing space for arboreal pythons.

to escape and makes it easy to clean/water/feed your snakes. Simply pull the box out from the shelf; you don't even have to figure out where to put the shoebox lid. However, this won't work for tiny hatchlings who can wriggle through even a ¼-inch gap, and some pythons will rub their noses raw in an effort to push through that gap.

Glass Terraria

The readily obtained glass aquariums are for most of us the simple way out. In the 20-gallon (76 L) or less size, they're relatively easy to move, easy to clean, and not very expensive. The screen tops that clip into place are sturdy enough to prevent escape for the smaller pythons. The larger all-glass tanks that are specifically designed for use as terraria have tops with sliding screened panels. A tank that measures 4 × 2 × 2 feet (1.2 × .61 × 1.2 m) is large enough for a 6- to 8-foot (1.8–2 m) long snake.

Cage height. This consideration comes into play for an arboreal python, such as the green tree python. Arboreal snakes need tree branches, and the caging needs to accommodate the height. With a few adjustments, standard aquaria/terraria can be adapted.

On the end. Consider turning a standard tank on its end, and gluing rubber feet (rubber stoppers work well) underneath. Add substrate and branches, clip a screen top onto the open side, and you've got a vertical format tank.

Stacking. If you remove the bottom from a standard 20-gallon (76 L) tank, you can stack that tank on top of a second tank. Secure the two together with 2-inch-wide (5 cm) package tape, add substrate, tree limbs, and a clip-on screen top, and you have a vertical tank large enough for a green tree python. Do not use a solid top; pythons (particularly the green tree python) need the ventilation and air flow afforded by a screen top.

Constructing a Stacked Tank

You'll need:
- two tanks of the same dimensions
- a hammer
- newspapers
- needle-nosed pliers
- wide packing tape
- heavy gloves

Safety glasses should be worn.

1. Put a pad of newspapers on a firm floor (cement or vinyl flooring), and put one tank on top of the pad.

2. Add another pad of newspapers inside the tank, extending slightly up the sides of the tanks. When you break the bottom out, you don't want stray bits of glass to fly upward and cut you.

3. Tap the bottom gently with a hammer until you hear it break, then tap along the perimeter of the tank.

4. Lift the newspaper and remove the glass as the pieces become loose. You may need to wiggle the pieces near the perimeter of the tank, so be careful that you don't cut yourself on a neighboring piece of glass.

5. Use the needle-nosed pliers to remove the last bits of glass at the edges.

6. Place the bottomless tank on top of the second tank and add a strip of wide packing tape across the back seam. Two shorter pieces of tape with folded-under pull tabs can be added on the sides.

When you place the stacked tanks in your snake room, put them about 6 inches (15 cm) from a wall. This will enable you to loosen the side tabs of tape and tilt the top tank back against the wall. This will make getting to the bottom of the lower tank for cleaning much easier.

Once the top tank has lost its bottom, it has lost much of its structural integrity and must be handled gently

Two aquariums can be stacked to provide a vertical cage.

until it is secured on top of the other tank.

Glass-fronted Boxes

These wooden cages are an older style of snake caging but one that is particularly good for larger snakes from a security viewpoint. They are generally made of ⅝-inch (16 mm) plywood, with a sliding or hinged glass front. The front is secured by a hasp, and ventilation holes are drilled in the sides, back, and top. The light is suspended from the top.

This type of caging can easily be made up to a floor area of 4 × 8 feet (1.2 × 2.4 m), the size of a single sheet of plywood. For the larger pythons—those up to 12 feet (3.65 m) —these cages work well. For these larger snakes, you might also think about lining the cage with a cabinet-quality mica; plywood, even with a varnish or painted finish, tends to absorb moisture and odor (the bigger the snake, the greater potential for the moisture or odor problems).

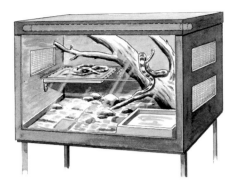

Larger pythons can be kept in glass-fronted wooden boxes, although these cages can be harder to clean than other types of caging.

For the snakes that need good air circulation, the plywood box type tends to be a little "close" unless special care is taken to add ventilation panels on the back, sides, and top. The dimensions of this type of cage—rather low and long—make it hard to set up any type of cage decoration or accessory. For the larger snakes, any type of cage decoration is temporary, because the weight and strength of these snakes simply moves it, knocks it down, or flattens it.

Ventilated plastic sweater-type boxes fit so snugly into the racks that lids are not needed; the shelf above serves as the top to each box.

Commercial Caging

Commercially made or custom cages are molded plastic or plastic laminate over plywood. Pet shops, herpetological societies, and national reptile magazines are resources you can use to locate commercially made cages.

These cages are easy to clean, come in a wide variety of sizes, and their uniform appearance gives a professional appearance to a reptile collection.

The Room-Sized Cage

Large pythons, like the reticulated and Burmese pythons over 10 feet (3 m) long, need a great deal of space. Snakes this large are generally too heavy and strong to keep in other cage types.

Many python keepers find it easiest to devote an entire room to their pet, simply because it simplifies feeding, cleaning, and watering. Such a room will need a climbing surface placed along one wall—cement blocks that are covered with enough cement to provide a roughened climbing surface work well. You'll need to seal all surfaces with a durable, waterproof surface. The floor can be bare cement, and the installation of a central drain will facilitate cleaning with a hose. Plan for adequate ventilation, either through heavily screened windows or a standard HVAC ductwork. If the idea of wafting the odor of your snake cage through your entire house bothers you, you can add a separate unit just for that room.

Hot spots. In addition to the temperature control afforded by the HVAC system, you'll need to add some heat/light lamps to provide a hot spot for your python. If you create a sturdy sunning shelf near the ceiling, you can aim the lights at that point. Be certain that the snake cannot get close enough to the light to burn itself. Your snake will need incandescent lighting for heating; fluorescent lights don't produce enough heat, and the ceramic heat lamps by themselves won't provide any light.

Water. The water bowl should be untippable and large enough for your snake to submerge itself—remember the incredible amount of water that can be displaced by a large python. Allow enough space between the level of the water and the top edge of the watering trough. You may chose to install a bathtub, complete with a water source and a drain, for your water container. Snakes often defecate in their water dish (particularly just after it has been cleaned), and you'll need an easy way to drain, clean, and refill it.

Food. Feeding a large python is easiest and safest if the snake is moved to a separate box for feeding. The snake then associates the box with food instead of associating the entrance of people into its cage with food.

If this isn't an option, feeding a large python will take two people—one to throw in the prekilled food, and a second to watch the python's reaction when it smells the food and detects the motion of its keeper in its cage. If you're going to change/clean the watering dish and feed your snake on the same day, clean the water bowl *before* you handle the food animals. Once that task is done, your entry into the cage a second time—this time smelling of food—will be safer.

Substrate

What you use on the floor of the cage is partially determined by the size of caging you select. For the ultra-simple sweater boxes used for the small pythons or the python babies, the substrate can be mulch, paper towels, or newspaper. For larger cages, mulch or newspapers work better than paper towels. For a room-

Commercially made plastic boxes and racks allow you to provide individualized housing for a lot of snakes in a fairly compact area.

Cages that can be co-joined are useful for the larger species; the cage's area can be increased as the snake grows.

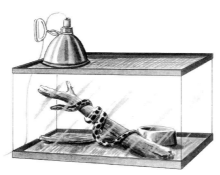

A simple heat light can provide lighting and warmth.

sized cage, leave the cement floor bare or add vinyl flooring.

Mulch (or wood shavings) gives the best purchase for crawling. It is absorbent enough to absorb liquid from the snake's stools or from an overturned water dish, and the small snakes may burrow into it if it's deep enough. You can spot clean simply by lifting out the debris. Every month or so, simply throw out the old mulch and replace it with new. It looks attractive, and you can add a few plants by burying the pots up to their rim in the mulch. The only caution with shavings or mulch is to avoid any form of cedar—cedar is loaded with phenols that are deadly to all reptiles (and amphibians, for that matter).

Paper towels are easy to replace when soiled, quickly absorb liquids, and make finding your snakes within

Paper towels and a log or rock for traction can make caging clean-up easy.

the cage easy. If you add a second folded towel in one half of the cage, the snake may utilize the folded portion as a hiding area. The downside is that paper towels don't afford much purchase for crawling, and they are too lightweight and rumple too easily to use in any cages larger than shoebox size. It is also difficult to make the cage look at all natural by adding plants or pieces of bark.

Newspaper is hard to beat for a substrate, especially for smaller pythons. It is very utilitarian and satisfactory for those who want a unadorned cage, and, when soiled, it is easily changed. It doesn't look particularly attractive, and the snakes will find crawling on it more difficult because it affords essentially no purchase. You may wish to start out with newspaper, but as time goes on, you probably will want to provide a more attractive environment for your snakes.

Note: Whether you use paper towels or newspapers, always add a small rock or piece of bark for "traction" purposes.

Indoor-outdoor carpeting is used by some keepers. Cut to the size of the cage, the carpet lies flat and looks attractive. However, it does tend to absorb fecal liquids. The difficulty lies in cleaning the carpet sections. Certainly you can shake off the dried debris, but the absorbed portion is going to smell. You can scrub the carpeting in your laundry sink or bathtub. (Be sure to clean and disinfect the sink when you are done.)

Our tip: Two substrates we do not recommend are kitty litter and corn cob bedding. Both are dusty. The kitty litter turns into clay mush when it gets wet, while the corn cob bedding tends to mold when dampened. It also expands when it gets damp and any ingested bedding can cause gut impactions in baby snakes.

Hide Boxes

When setting up your cages, you need to provide adequate hiding areas for your snakes and this is best done by removable hide boxes, which make cleaning much easier. It is always best to provide more than one hide box, one near the cage's hot spot and one further away, at the cooler end of the cage.

Plastic hide boxes can be purchased at your local pet store, or you can buy a dark plastic box, cut an entry hole along the rim, and turn the box upside down in the cage. Cardboard boxes work as well, but because they can't be washed you'll need to replace them every few months. The dark plastic boxes with the lids left on and an access hole cut through the lid make excellent humidity chambers for those species that seem to prefer a more humid environment. You can mix dampened wood shavings and sphagnum moss together to make the hide box more humid. Place the moist box away from the hot spot. Again, you need to give your python a choice by providing a dry hide box, so it won't always be forced to rest in a damp box.

For climbing pythons, buy a box that has a wide lip around the rim (like a dishpan), cut an access hole at the rim, and mount the box on the ceiling of the cage. This is done simply by screwing in a series of very sturdy L-pins (obtainable at a hardware store) to form tracks and sliding the rim of the box into the track. In this setting, pythons will feel secure and will rest with their head out of the entry hole, surveying the cage below.

Cage Humidity

Cage humidity can be an important consideration in successful maintenance. Pythons from humid areas, like the green tree pythons, will develop skin problems and have trouble shed-

Pythons will feel more secure if they have a hide box in their cage.

ding if the humidity in the cage is too low. Aridland python species, like the Stimson's python, languish if kept under too humid conditions.

One of the easiest ways to control humidity in your cages is by judicious size of the water dish. Certainly all pythons need to have clean drinking water at all times, but a smaller dish in the cages of aridland pythons will help keep the humidity level down. If there is a heat tape or heating pad under part of the cage, make sure the water bowl is at the far end for the aridland species. For pythons from humid areas, a larger water bowl will help maintain optimum humidity levels. A light misting of the snake, using a spray bottle with tepid water, may also assist in the shedding process.

Cleaning the Cage without Getting Bitten

Pythons can be belligerent at times. It just seems that sometimes they awaken with a king-sized Excedrin headache and lash out at any- and everything. The mood might quickly pass, or it may linger; it seems as if only the python knows.

With some pythons the mood never entirely leaves. Sometimes these moods occur when they are least expected and least wanted—for instance, during cage cleaning.

Certainly the best way to clean a python's cage thoroughly and safely is to remove the python while you work. And, the best way to move pythons, at least those up to 8 or 9 feet (2.4–2.7 m) in length, is with a snake hook.

The python can be "hooked" and placed in a covered container (we use 40- to 60-gallon [151–227 L] plastic trash cans) while the cage is cleaned, disinfected (don't use a phenol-based cleanser!), rinsed, and dried. The snake hook is again employed to remove the snake from the container and replace it in its cage. And then we all know what happens: The snake, disturbed and with its metabolism correspondingly raised, defecates in the freshly cleaned cage and the whole procedure must begin again!

Sometimes, cleaning a python's cage, no matter the size of the animal, can be simple and straightforward, especially if the snake is resting in a hide box or is tightly coiled in a soaking tub. Merely cover the front of the box or the top of the tub and go about the business of cleaning. There may be those times, however, when the snake is actively watching you with a level of attention that is different than usual. If that is the case, and if it is possible to do so, delay the cleaning.

If it is not possible to delay, use a solid baffle of some type to contain the snake. Even then, if it is a big snake, use extreme care. And, how big is big? In our estimation, any python that is 8 feet (2.4 m) long or more is big, and those that are upwards of 10 feet (3 m) are very big! No matter how well you know the python, cleaning the cage should be considered a two-person job—one to clean after the other has contained the snake (most pythons will readily enter a hide box where they can be contained through the cleaning) or diverted its attention.

Use care and respect whenever working with these snakes. Do not become a statistic.

General Husbandry

Heat

Since all pythons occur in tropical or subtropical environments, captive temperatures will play a big role in keeping your snake healthy and in stimulating reproduction. Most reptile keepers who have a collection of snakes will usually devote a spare bedroom to them and heat that room preferentially rather than heating the individual cages. While heating the entire room gives you less flexibility in controlling temperature, you can instead decide to control the temperature of each individual cage.

Individual cage heat can be provided by placing a heating pad on the substrate or underneath the cage, or by mounting radiant heat lamps from above. Keep in mind when setting up your cages that most heating pads can become dangerously hot if trapped between two surfaces that do not allow the built-up heat to escape or dissipate. If you are placing an entire heating pad beneath a cage, the cage should be elevated above the pad, using 1 × 1 (2.5 × 2.5 cm) lumber strips, to allow adequate ventilation. We often place one end of the cage over part of the heating pad, leaving half of the pad open. If the heating pad is placed inside a cage, we put the heating pad on top of a hide box. The snake can sit on top of the heating pad or crawl into the hide box beneath the heating pad, but again, one side of the heating pad is open to the air and is well ventilated.

Note: Prevent overheating. Both heating pads and heat lamps will work but both should have thermostats to control the temperature and prevent overheating the cage. In an ideal cage there would be a warm spot and enough room for the snake to move to a cooler area so it will have some choice in selecting its temperature. This freedom to thermoregulate is important; in the wild, a python can simply move off to a cooler spot or choose a sunny spot to warm up in. In your caging, you need to provide the same options.

Always keep in mind the placement of hide boxes in relationship to your cage's hot spot. Sometimes your python's urge to hide may be stronger

The ready availability of carpet pythons, including this prettily marked jungle carpet (Morelia spilota cheynei) *may be attributed to the ease with which they are captive bred.*

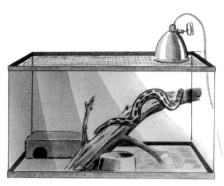

Provide a thermal gradient in your cage by use of a lamp.

than its desire to select the best temperature for whatever activity is going on. Having hide boxes in both the warmest and the coolest parts of the cage gives your snake both security and a choice in temperature.

Temperatures

Daytime temperatures should range between 85 and 90°F (29–33°C). The nighttime temperature should be allowed to drop to 75 to 78°F (24–26°C) by attaching a timer to your heat source, or by installing a commercially made thermostat in your cage that has both day and night settings.

Lighting

Lighting can be provided by either incandescent bulbs or fluorescent lighting. Some of the more expensive fluorescents that match the spectrum of sunlight emit light that makes both plants and animals more vibrantly colored. Bulbs of this type will make any plants in the cage healthier, but this type of lighting does not seem necessary for snakes. We have seen perfectly healthy pythons that have been raised under incandescent lighting all of their lives, and the same can be said for fluorescent lighting.

Altering Day Length

You may want to alter the length of your day and night cycles if you are trying to breed your snakes. Many breeders will reduce the winter cycle to eight or nine hours of light and allow the summer cycle to build up to sixteen hours of light. You can check and record the sunrise/sunset times in the weather section of your local paper, so you'll have a daily log to use for reference. Another way is to alter the daily cycle by five minutes a day or 30 minutes a week to mimic daylight changes.

There are some unanswered questions about how important day length is to the breeding cycle; temperature seems to play a more important role. Those breeders who change their cycles are not sure if it helps, but they assume that it may be useful and certainly it does not hurt anything. We have been very successful in breeding pythons in the Pacific Northwest without altering our usual 12–12 day/night split, and we have been successful in breeding pythons in Florida when we did alter the day/night cycles to match the seasons.

Mixing Species

Most serious python breeders will try to pair up their snakes and breed them. The only time different species or genera of snakes would be housed together would be if the breeders were trying to hybridize them, such as crossing a carpet with a diamond python. If you are keeping pythons just for the enjoyment of dealing with beautiful creatures, there are some species that could be mixed without worry about crossbreeding, such as the green tree python and carpet python, or the Burmese python and the African rock python.

What Not to Mix

There are some species of pythons that should never be mixed with other pythons (or indeed, with any other type of snakes) because of cannibalistic tendencies. These are the black-headed python, ringed python, white-lipped python, and the water python.

We are especially reluctant to house different species of pythons together if the snakes have come out of the wild. For one thing, snakes that come from widely separated parts of the world are often exposed to bacteria and parasites that are very distinct for their own area. Therefore, you run the risk of exposing your snakes to a whole set of new bacteria and parasites against which they have no resistance.

Even caging two of the same type of pythons together can cause problems, due to feeding. We have always preferred to keep our pythons one to a cage so we can control the amount of food they eat and not have to worry about two snakes fighting over the same meal.

Feeding

The Mechanics of Feeding

Pythons are largely scent-oriented snakes, meaning that they use their sense of smell more than sight or feel to find their prey. This reliance on scent can work for you in feeding your pet. For example, you can give a familiar scent to an unfamiliar food item—such as a frozen-thawed lab mouse—by rubbing its nose with a lizard or bird, so that your snake will eat the new food.

Scent cues can also work against you. For example, if you forget to wash your hands and change clothing after handling a food item and then try to handle your snake. If you smell like a mouse, your snake may well assume you are a mouse. During the breeding season of early spring or late winter, you may handle one male, fail to wash your hands of the pheromones that

If food is placed just outside a hide box, the snake will frequently feed when the house is quiet and no one is around.

both male and female snakes give off at this time, then try to handle a second male. Beware! Your snake may assume you are a rival male. "Food" or "rival," you may be bitten.

The scent molecules in its surroundings are carried by the python's tongue into the mouth, where they are transferred to the Jacobson's organ in the palate (see the Glossary, page 93). There the odors are sorted into basic categories of food or sex: Male or female? Danger? Meaningless odor? Then behaviors appropriate to the scents are carried out.

Pythons are constricting snakes. They grasp their prey item in their mouths and then throw loops either over the item or around it. Smaller prey items may simply be pinned

Offering prekilled food on a pair of forceps reduces your chance of being bitten.

Although captive white-lipped pythons (Leiopython albertisii) *feed readily upon rodents, they can be cannibalistic.*

prey. The constrictions will become perfunctory or bypassed altogether; swallowing may begin immediately.

To swallow, the python generally seeks out the nose of its prey item and then proceeds to engulf it, moving each side of its mouth forward over the prey item. Once the item is inside the mouth and throat, progressive, rearward constriction of the muscles of the throat forces the item down into the stomach of the snake. Digestion may be slow or rapid, depending on the snake, the time of year, and the ambient temperature, but the bulge in the snake made by the prey item generally disappears within a week. During this time the snake is less active than usual, moving only as necessary. A python that is handled at this time, even on a hook, may regurgitate its food.

How Often to Feed

Pythons, despite their size, are like all other snakes in that they don't need much food. Feed your python every three to six weeks. During the breeding season, both males and females may go off-feed. Gravid females may cease feeding as the time to lay their eggs approaches. During the winter cooling period, feeding may also stop.

What to Feed

Diet items for your python will generally be warmblooded items. Offer prekilled lab mice and rats, gerbils, and chicks to the smaller pythons—those less than 8 feet (2.4 meters) long. Larger pythons need bigger food items, such as rabbits and whole chickens.

Most pet stores offer frozen mice and rats, and there are rodent breeding companies that offer frozen feeder mice and rats in larger quantities (usually in counts of 50). You may be able to purchase live rats and mice from individuals who breed them for their

down while they are swallowed. A larger item—something as large as a rat or rabbit—will be constricted until it suffocates; then it will be swallowed. When you feed prekilled items, whether mice or rabbits, after a number of feedings the snake will figure out that it doesn't need to constrict the

Guided both by scent and motion, the brown water python (Liasis fuscus) *is an effective predator.*

own snakes but have extras available. You can use these live rodents to set up your own breeding colonies, but we have found that the odor and work involved is more than we want to deal with.

Thawing frozen food items is easy and takes surprisingly little time. We thaw them in warm water (a half hour for mice and rats) and blot them dry. Then we use a long pair of forceps to offer a mouse or rat to each of the smaller pythons. Generally, it only takes a few feedings for the pythons to catch on to the process and to eagerly accept the food items. Occasionally we need to tease a snake by gently tapping on its nose with the food item and then slightly withdrawing it. If the snake does not grasp the item after the second tap, we withdraw the food and try again in two weeks. You may wish to leave the food just outside the hide box.

To feed a larger python, we transfer the snake to a feeding box—a secure plywood box with ventilation panels— and close the lid. Then we bring the thawed food item to the box and open the lid enough to throw in the food item. Remember that a snake larger than 10 feet (3 m) needs two people to be safely handled. If providing a feeding box is not an option, two peo-ple are especially needed to feed a larger python: one to open the cage and throw in the food, the other to watch the snake and intervene if necessary.

If the larger python does not begin to feed within a few minutes, open the feeding box. Using a baffle to protect yourself from the snake (we use the screen top from a terrarium or a piece of lightweight plywood), remove the food item, return the snake to its cage, and try feeding again in two weeks. For those pythons fed in their own cages, again, use a baffle to protect yourself while you remove the food.

The African rock python, Python sebae, *feeds readily on prekilled rats. Until the snake becomes accustomed to prekilled food, it will constrict the rat before eating it.*

The burrowing python, Calabaria reinhardtii, *often kills its prey by pressing it against the walls of its burrow.*

Using Wild Prey

When you begin to add up the cost of feeder mice, rats, or rabbits, feeding wild mammals seems a lot more attractive than buying the domestic kinds. If you have an abundance of wild prey, you can offer it to your python. Be certain that your wild-caught mouse or rat hasn't ingested any rodent poisons. Be aware that wild populations can carry diseases that are transmittable to humans. (The deadly hantavirus, for instance, is found in deer mouse populations in the western states.) The third point is a practical one. Once they've tasted wild rodents, some pythons like them so much that they refuse to accept the domestic kinds again. We breed white-footed mice especially for snakes that will not accept lab mice.

Breeding Your Own Food Rodents

Some people find it easier to breed their own rodents for snake food. They can be easily bred, but will do best if kept at room temperature (meaning indoors) to avoid the heat of summer or the coldness of winter. If not kept indoors, breeding may stop or the adults may eat the babies.

Mice are the most easily bred. Three females and one male can be kept in a ten-gallon tank with a substrate of wood shavings (don't use cedar), a food dish, and a water bottle. Two or three colonies will provide a steady supply of babies which can be killed, frozen, and later fed to hatchling snakes. Or the young can be moved to another cage after weaning and allowed to grow to feed to your adult snakes. If you breed your own mice and rats, you'll need to kill them before freezing them or offering them to your snakes. To humanely kill a mouse or rat, hold the animal by its tail and swing it so that its head hits sharply against the edge of a counter or table top. Gentleness is not the key word here; you want death to be very fast.

Medical Problems

If you keep animals for any length of time, you'll encounter some kind of medical problems. With exotic animals like pythons it is very important to locate a veterinarian who has had experience with reptiles, and establish a good relationship with him or her. Look for a veterinarian who will listen to you, query you about your snake's environmental requirements, and then explain how those conditions might relate to the medical problem in question. Some people try to avoid veterinarians because of the cost involved, but we feel this is very short-sighted. As many years as we have been keeping reptiles, we have regularly relied upon (and welcomed) the help and expertise of our veterinarians.

Finding a Veterinarian

The first place to start looking for a veterinarian is your telephone book. Look under Veterinarians in the yellow pages; some veterinarians advertise their specialties with a display ad. Or call your local pet store and ask for the name of the veterinarian who takes care of their reptiles. Also, ask other reptile keepers in your area for the names of veterinarians they have used, or check the on-line services and the Internet for veterinarians' names.

Once you've narrowed your search (and you may have only one or two to choose from), call the veterinarians in question and talk to them about their experience. When there are a couple of veterinarians in a single practice, make sure that the one you want is scheduled to work the day of your appointment.

Veterinarians are trained in the use of medications and are the ones to prescribe medicines and their dosages. We have listed usual dosages later in this chapter, simply as starting points for medications that your veterinarian may not have used extensively.

Quarantining Your Snake

The most important thing you can do to protect the health of your python collection is to quarantine incoming animals for a month, in a room apart from the room where your collection is kept. This isolation is very important, because some snake diseases are highly infectious *and* fatal.

When a new snake arrives, remove it from the bag and examine it closely. Make certain it is the sex you ordered (see Sexing, pages 46–47). Look for any wounds and check the snake's mouth to make sure it is pink-white and free from any cheesy areas of

Put your new python in quarantine until you're certain it won't bring any new pathogens into your collection.

A simple stick-on thermometer will let you know at a glance if the cage temperature is right.

debris. Look closely for snake mites. We always examine the bag that held the snake, as the little black mites will show up well against the white cloth. This bag should be washed and dried (preferably in an electric or gas dryer, as the heat helps kill any mites) before being used for any other snakes.

1. Place your snake in a clean cage with fresh water and a hide box. Provide a hot spot, and keep the rest of the cage from 80 to 87°F (27–30°C) during the day and 75 to 85°F (24–29°C) at night.

2. Wait at least 24 hours before offering prekilled food.

3. During the next two or three weeks, watch for any signs of mites. A mite infestation may be indicated by the snake soaking in its water bowl for protracted periods, the snake twitching its skin nervously, or by swollen areas under the snake's belly scutes. The mites themselves are visible to your naked eye, especially near the snake's eyes.

4. Watch your snake as it crawls. Does it have any difficulty in crawling? Does it flick its tongue as it crawls? (See the section on inclusion body disease, page 39, if your snake has trouble crawling, or if it contorts its neck or seems to stare into space, and be forewarned: These are serious symptoms.)

5. Examine your snake's stools. A healthy snake has stools that are approximately half solid and half liquid, half dark and half white. Take a sample stool to your veterinarian, so he or she can check for parasites. If your newly arrived snake has not fed, the easiest way to get a stool specimen is to give the snake a bath in tepid water. If this does not work, it may be possible to obtain enough fecal material for an exam by gently manipulating the cloacal area while you massage the ventral surface of the snake toward the vent. Your veterinarian can assist with this procedure if you need help.

6. After a month's time, if your snake has eaten at least once, has normal-looking stools, does not look thin, and shows absolutely no sign of mites, you can incorporate the snake into your collection.

The Warm Cage

If you have a medical problem with one of your snakes, you need to be able to isolate this snake in a cage where the temperature can be elevated. Studies have shown that sick or injured snakes will deliberately seek out higher temperature and that this seems to help them recover. When you are dealing with a respiratory problem, with an injury, or with mouth rot, you should always be prepared to provide a *warm cage.*

Temperature

The most effective temperature seems to be a constant 90°F (32.2°C) both day and night. This should be maintained for a week or ten days, or as long as your snake is on medication. Be certain that plenty of clean drinking water is available.

Antibiotics and Culturing

When your snake has an abscess, mouth rot, or a respiratory problem, using a warm cage can speed recovery even before medication is begun. Your veterinarian may want to start a course of antibiotics.

Try culturing. There is a way to more effectively determine which antibiotics to use, but it requires some forethought on your part. Ask your veterinarian for some sterile culture tubes. Keep them tightly stoppered in your refrigerator until you need them. When you notice your snake has an abscess, mouth rot, or trouble breathing, put it in the warm cage, but just before you do this, touch a cotton swab to the affected area, and then roll the swab across the culture media. For a respiratory problem, dab up a bit of the mucus in the snake's mouth. Take the tube to your veterinarian so the bacteria can be incubated and tested for sensitivity to different antibiotics.

It will take a few days for the results of the culture to come back and by then your snake may have improved due to heat therapy. The advantage is that if antibiotic therapy is needed, your veterinarian knows what type to use. Perhaps you are able to decide if immediate medical intervention or heat therapy is the best course of action, but experience and a good veterinarian can help you make those decisions.

Shedding

Snake shedding is one of the most useful indicators of what is going on with your captive python. It gives you distinct clues about reproductive cycles, parasite infestations, illness, and general health. There are some very specific times in your python's life during which sheds will occur; they can provide you with some useful information if you can interpret them correctly:

1. The first time a snake sheds is a few days after hatching; the sheds

Innoculate a culture tube with suspected pathogens to test for antibiotic sensitivity.

should then occur fairly regularly throughout your snake's growth to adulthood. The first sign of an impending shed is when the snake's eyes turn a milky blue. After a few days, the eyes return to their usual color, but the skin dulls. Within a week, the snake will rub its nose against a rock or branch to loosen the skin at the lips. Then the snake will crawl out of its old skin. Make certain that the snake's eye caps have been shed. If they haven't, gently remove them from the snake's eyes with a pair of tweezers.

Newly-hatched baby pythons generally shed before feeding.

If your python is having trouble shedding, soak it in lukewarm (or room temperature) water for a half-hour or so to help soften the old skin.

Misting or soaking a small python may assist in shedding.

2. Once the snake has reached adulthood, the sheds take on more significance. **Reproductive sheds** will occur following a cooling period, just prior to ovulation. The snake will shed again in several weeks (the **pre-egg-laying shed**), and once more after laying the eggs (the **post-egg-laying shed**). These are all useful indicators that will be discussed in the breeding section (see pages 40–52).

3. Aside from the predictable sheds mentioned above, your python should have a fairly uniform rate of shedding under normal, non-breeding circumstances. Sheds outside the normal periods should always be evaluated for possible causes. Blister disease, manifested by raised blisters on the skin, is caused by quarters that are too damp. Frequent shedding is the snake's way of dealing with excessive humidity. If snake mites get into your collection and infest a snake, the snake's response is to initiate a shed. Injuries to the skin, such as burns, will also initiate more frequent sheds during the healing process.

4. Other health problems can stimulate frequent sheds. If you have a snake that is shedding frequently and doesn't look quite right to you, take it to your veterinarian for a general examination. It would also be wise to bring a stool specimen with you for this examination.

External Parasites

Ticks are blood-sucking, teardrop-shaped arachnids that can sometimes be found on pythons, mouthparts firmly attached between the scales around the eyes or near the head. These parasites are easy to see, because they measure from ⅛ to ¼ inch (3.2–6.4 mm) across and are dark brown or gray in color. They aren't particularly attractive, but in small numbers they don't generally represent a serious health hazard. Researchers are still undecided whether ticks are a vector in inclusion body disease (see page 39), so prompt removal of these parasites is recommended.

When you find a tick on your snake, use a pair of tweezers to grasp the parasite by its head, and with a steady but firm pressure, pull it off the snake. Don't pull it sharply, because you want to remove the entire creature, not only its body. After you remove the tick, you can swab the bite site with a bit of alcohol or other disinfectant. Check your python in a week or so for any ticks you may have missed the first time, and remove them.

Mites are more of a problem than ticks, because they are smaller, harder to eradicate and have been implicated in the spread of some serious snake diseases. The blood loss alone, caused by a heavy infestation, can weaken and kill a snake.

Mite infestations can be detected partly by the behavior of the snake. A snake with mites is restless and will sometimes rub against the sides of its cage to try and dislodge the little burrowing arachnids. The snake will soak in its water dish to try to drown the mites. It may go into a shed to try to get rid of them, but none of these actions will work in the confines of a cage unless you lend a hand. You need to not only get the mites off the snakes—which is comparatively easy—but you have to eliminate the mites from all the nooks and crannies in the cage. If you have mites in one cage, you need to take immediate action to prevent their spread to your entire collection:

1. Clean the cage. Cages that have mites in them should be taken out of your snake room, stripped of all decorations, thoroughly cleaned (use a dilute bleach solution and a scrub brush, at the very least), and left empty for a few weeks while they are sprayed repeatedly with a mite killer or exposed to a heavy dosage of a No-Pest insecticide strip.

2. Replace cage accessories with new accessories that you are certain are mite-free after you are sure that your cage itself has been completely cleaned. We once tried to eradicate mites from a section of cholla cactus skeleton that we particularly liked. We dunked it in boiling water, left it in our freezer for a week, then slow-roasted it in the oven at 250°F (121°C). Once it cooled, we put it back in the cage, but a week later we noticed the mites were back. At that point we figured that the cage had not been properly cleaned, so we went to work again and cleaned the cage, repeated our cleaning of the cholla, and treated the cage inhabitants once again. The problem did not reoccur.

3. If there are mites on your snake, consult your veterinarian or ask at a

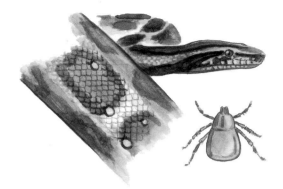

Ticks are visible problems that are fairly easy to eliminate from a collection or from an individual snake.

pet shop. Most pet shops carry specific products made to kill mites on reptiles, but there are a few insecticides made for general use that will also work. Mites can become resistant to any insecticide if used long enough, so it is best to do a thorough job of eliminating them the first time.

4. No-Pest strips are probably the easiest miticide to use. Cut a piece off (the surface of the strip is oily-feeling and a serrated blade seems to cut the strip faster) and use a couple of twist-ties to hang the piece near the top of the cage. A piece that is 1 × 2 inches (2.5 × 5.1 cm) will be large enough for a 20-gallon-sized (76 L) enclosure. If your cage has a screen top, you can simply lay the piece on top of the screen. In either case, remove the water dish when you use No-Pest, because the volatile pesticide emitted from the strip will contaminate any water left in the cage.

Leave the strip in place for about a week, then remove the strip, clean the cage, replace the water, and wait another week. Repeat the process. (This second treatment nails the mite eggs that were unaffected by the strip but that have hatched since then.)

5. You can also use a product called Nix, which is primarily used to kill human body lice. Nix can be purchased at any drugstore. This is a concentrated cream rinse; add 2 ounces (57 g) of the rinse to ¾ gallon (2.8 L) of room-temperature water and shake or stir until it is mixed. Put the solution into a sprayer.

Remove the cage furniture from the cage and plan to replace it with new items once the treatment has ended. Also remove the water dish from the cage and spray the entire cage. Wipe the snake down with the solution, using a sprayed cotton swab to wipe around the snake's eyes (a snake quite obviously cannot close its eyes against the spray).

Let the cage dry for the rest of the day and then replace the water. Put in a temporary hide box (and new perching branches if your python is an arboreal species). Repeat this entire process in a week, being certain to remove the water dish during the treatment. Once the cage has dried, put in the new, mite-free accessories and replace the water dish.

6. If you are keeping some of the smaller pythons and don't want to use insecticides on your snake, place the snake in a shallow container of water for a few hours to drown the majority of the mites. We have used a 5-gallon (19 L) bucket, with holes poked through the lid, or a plastic aquarium with the plastic snap-on lid. After soaking (the snake will move around in the container, both below and above the water during this time), remove the snake, dry it, and give it a light coating of cooking oil or mineral oil. Pay particular attention to the area around the eyes and under the chin, both places where mites like to hide. The oil will help suffocate the mites, and after an hour or two you can wipe your snake down and return it to its cage, which you have cleaned, sprayed, and dried in the interim.

Remember: Prevention is easier than eradication with mite infestations. The best solution is to examine any new snake very carefully and to deal with any mite problem before the snake is added to your collection.

Internal Parasites

Symptoms. If your python is thin and not gaining weight or has loose foul-smelling stools, it should be tested for internal parasites. This is particularly true if your python was wild-caught.

Diagnosis. You need to know specifically what parasite(s) are involved. Obtain a fresh stool specimen and take it to your veterinarian. If you are dealing with an animal that has come out of the wild, discuss treatment choices with your veterinarian. Your snake may have several types of internal parasites, and it may be sensible to give several parasiticides at once. Experience has shown us that the sudden killing of several types of parasites can cause more problems than the parasites themselves. It is probably wise to follow a conservative course, treating for one type of parasite at a time and then giving a resting period before treating for another.

Diagnosis and Treatment of Endoparasites

Because of the difficulties in identifying endoparasites and the necessity to administer purge dosages by the weight of the snake, ridding your snake of internal parasites is best left to a qualified reptile veterinarian. The presence of the following tables is in no way intended to promote home diagnoses and medications. They should be considered only as they are intended, as a guideline. Below are a few of the recommended medications and dosages.

Amoebas and Trichomonads: 40–50 mg/kg of Metronidazole orally.

The treatment is repeated in two weeks.

Dimetridazole can also be used but the dosage is very different: 40–50 mg/kg of Dimetrizadole is administered daily for five days. The treatment is then repeated in two weeks. All treatments with both medications are administered once daily.

Coccidia: Many treatments are available.

The dosages of sulfadiazine, sulfamerazine, and sulfamethazine are identical. Administer 75 mg/kg the first day, then follow up for the next five days with 45 mg/kg. All treatments orally and once daily.

Sulfadimethoxine is also effective. The initial dosage is 90 mg/kg orally to be followed on the next five days with 45 mg/kg orally. All dosages are administered once daily.

Trimethoprim-sulfa may also be used: 30 mg/kg should be administered once daily for seven days.

Cestodes (Tapeworms): Several effective treatments are available.

Bunamidine may be administered orally at a dosage of 50 mg/kg. A second treatment occurs in 14 days.

Niclosamide, orally, at a dosage of 150 mg/kg, is also effective. A second treatment is given in two weeks.

Praziquantel may be administered either orally or intramuscularly. The dosage is 5–8 mg/kg and is to be repeated in 14 days.

Trematodes (Flukes): Praziquantel at 8 mg/kg may be administered either orally or intramuscularly. The treatment is repeated in 2 weeks.

Nematodes (Roundworms): Several effective treatments are available.

Levamisole, an injectable intraperitoneal treatment, should be administered at a dosage of 10 mg/kg and the treatment repeated in two weeks.

Ivermectin, injected intramuscularly in a dosage of 200 mcg/kg is effective. The treatment is to be repeated in two

weeks. Ivermectin can be toxic to certain taxa.

Thiabendazole and Fenbendazole have similar dosages. Both are administered orally at 50–100 mg/kg and repeated in 14 days.

Mebendazole is administered orally at a dosage of 20–25 mg/kg and repeated in 14 days.

Respiratory Problems

Respiratory problems are often bacterial in origin and in the early stages can be diagnosed simply by an excess of mucus in the snake's mouth. A snake that is literally drooling is in big trouble. Less severe cases can be noticed when the snake rubs its face against the glass front of its enclosure and leaves a wet smear, or when the snake holds its mouth slightly ajar. In severe cases, the snake may hold its head elevated and a pocket of mucus will form, causing a bulge in the throat. The snake will make a gurgling or raspy sound when it tries to breathe. This is not a comfortable situation for your python.

Causes. Respiratory problems are usually triggered by stress, possibly a severe mite infestation, or sometimes improper cage temperatures. Occasionally, the stress of reproduction can trigger this problem.

Treatments. If the problem appears to be severe, don't wait—take your snake to the veterinarian. A hot water bottle packed with your snake will help maintain a safe warmth if the outside temperatures are below 70°F (21°C).

If the problem is not acute, you can begin treatment on your own. The first step is to elevate the cage temperature, which may enable your snake to fight off the infection. If the snake doesn't look better in a day's time, take a throat culture specimen to your veterinarian. A cotton swab, rolled in some of the mucus in the snake's mouth or throat, will enable the veterinarian to culture the causative agent.

Regurgitation

There are both environmental and internal causes of regurgitation; sometimes the two can play off each other. The environmental causes are straightforward, like feeding too much at a time, handling after feeding, or letting the cage cool too much after feeding. Keeping the cage too warm is another cause.

Regurgitation can also be caused by a bloom of intestinal flora. Normally present, intestinal flora can, under stressful conditions, increase to pathogenic numbers.

• Wild-caught animals undergo a lot of stress in getting from their home to yours. The conditions of capture may be difficult; the python is generally noosed and then forced into a small bag that is knotted next to the snake's tightly bunched body. After several days, or a week or two, the snake is dumped from the bag into a large container (metal cattle troughs with screened lids are typical) with other snakes. Temperature maintenance is uncertain at best, and water may or may not be offered. After a few more weeks the snake is re-bagged and shipped to a wholesaler, or perhaps directly to you. A snake with normal gut flora and feeding response would be a rarity under these conditions.

• A captive-born python can experience this same sort of problem when stressed by shipping, exposure to another snake with regurgitation syndrome, or by changes in its environment too subtle for its keeper to pick up on.

Treatment. Whether wild-caught or captive-hatched, the beginning treatment is the same. Place the snake in a warm, quiet cage for a week or so and offer smaller meals, both in the number of mice, mice or chicks, and in the size of the individual food animals. If the problem continues, take the python and a stool specimen to your veterinarian.

Mouth Rot

Mouth rot is a catchall term for any infectious disease of the mouth. A more technical term is *infectious stomatitus*, which lets you know that the problem is infectious and can be transmitted to other snakes. The *stomatitus* portion means literally inflammation of the mouth or stoma. There may be several different causes.

Symptoms. You may first realize there is a problem when you see that your snake cannot close its mouth.

Diagnosis. When you hold the snake and gently open its mouth (use both hands for this, the fingers of one hand to catch the throat skin and pull it down, while holding the upper jaw with your thumb and forefinger of the other hand), you may be able to see lines of cheesy-looking material next to the teeth in either the upper or lower jaw. The lining of the mouth may be red and discolored. Certainly this problem needs to be treated.

Treatment. Try lifting out the cheesy material, using a cotton swab dipped in water or dipped in a very dilute saline solution. Apply Polysporin ointment to the affected areas with a cotton swab. (Polysporin ointment and

Polysporin cream can be purchased at your drugstore without a prescription; the ointment is oil-based and tends to cling better than the cream.) Elevate the cage temperature for a week to ten days. Check and treat the mouth daily until the signs are gone.

If the cheesy material does not come away cleanly, or if the mouth is red and discolored and bleeding, you need veterinarian assistance with this problem. Again, use a warm cage during treatment with any prescribed medications.

Viral and Retroviral Problems

As with humans, there is no effective python treatment for viral or retroviral problems. Retroviruses are very minute, just larger than virus-sized bits of pathogenic DNA, and they are so new to reptile medicine as to be successfully identified only at necropsy. Both viral and retroviral infections are diagnosed partially by symptoms and partly by the lack of response to any treatment.

Inclusion Body Disease

This is a fatal disease characterized by regurgitation, followed by central nervous system (CNS) disorders (including head tremors and the inability of the snake to right itself if turned over). The snake also loses the ability to focus its eyes and exhibits a characteristic upward-staring behavior called star gazing.

A python that twists over and seems to stare upwards exhibits unfavorable symptoms characteristic of inclusion body disease (IBD).

The disease is thought to be caused by a retrovirus, and is probably transmitted by mites. The name, inclusion body disease (IBD), was coined when captive snakes began to display what are now classic CNS problems and subsequently died, and the only out-of-the-ordinary finding was scattered dark areas or inclusion bodies inside body cells.

IBD can spread though your entire collection and there is no treatment and no cure. The only effective control is through the quarantine of incoming animals and the immediate humane killing and sanitary disposal of the remains.

Breeding

One of the most challenging yet satisfying experiences in python keeping occurs when you succeed in actually getting your pythons to reproduce. For many python keepers, this is the ultimate measure of husbandry skills and a major source of income. Even if you choose not to breed your animals, however, learning about the mechanics and behaviors involved will help you better understand your own snake's actions, especially during what is normally considered the breeding season.

In the Northern Hemisphere, breeding season coincides with the shortest days of the year, December to April. A few species breed in the fall, but the majority of pythons in our hemisphere

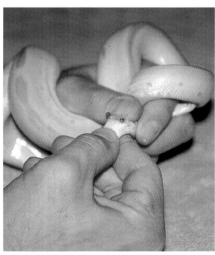

With some baby male pythons, you can roll your thumb gently across the tail base to evert the hemipenes.

breed during the winter. As with the captive reproduction of any animal, a certain amount of preparation is needed before the animals can be placed together, whether the placement occurs in December, January, February, or March. During this preparation time, you may also wish to plan on how you will house, feed, monitor, and sell/give away anywhere from 10 to 60 young.

Sexual Maturity

The next step after sexing your python is to determine that your animals are sexually mature and in good enough condition to withstand the rigors of breeding. Sexual maturity appears to be a function of size rather than age, and with some exception most pythons can reproduce when two-thirds to three-quarters grown. Young males do not need to be as large as females; indeed, with some species, mature males will not grow to the same size as the females. For Burmese pythons, for instance, males can successfully breed at about 8 feet (2.4 m) in length, whereas the females rarely breed before reaching 10 feet (3 m) in length.

With young breeders you will often get smaller clutches of eggs than in older, more mature animals. If your young animal has undergone a very rapid period of growth just prior to breeding, there is more stress and risk to the female.

Many people try to get their snakes to breeding size in the shortest possible time, and breed them at the youngest size possible. The incidence of reproductive failure is much higher for these younger snakes, and most breeders prefer not to "push" their female snakes this way.

Hefty Is Good

Another cause of reproductive failure, as evidenced by infertile or retained eggs, is by trying to breed snakes that are not in good physical condition. The female especially needs to have good fat reserves and good body weight to produce a viable clutch of eggs. Remember that the female will not feed from the time she becomes gravid until she lays the eggs. If she is permitted to incubate the eggs herself, she will not feed during the incubation period. After deposition or incubation, putting that lost weight back on the female can be a difficult task. Males will stop feeding during the breeding season, so they also need to begin the season at good weight.

Cycling to Induce Breeding

Getting Ready

Although there may be some courtship or attempts at copulation during various times of the year if the sexes are placed together, most of these encounters will not result in viable eggs if the snakes have not been properly cycled. *Cycling* used in this sense means a progression of climactic factors, such as increasing day lengths, gentle misting, and day/night temperature fluctuations, that duplicate the day/night and rain cycles in the snake's area of origin. This triggers the reproduction center in the pineal area in the brain, which in turns sends "wake up—it's time to reproduce" signals to the ovaries and testes.

Not all pythons require cycling; ball pythons and Burmese pythons have been known to reproduce at odd times of the year under captive conditions.

Timing

For those python species that do need cycling, most python keepers begin the process during the early winter, usually November and December. It is important to pick a time and then stay with that same cycle year after year. It is also useful to learn a bit about the natural history of the snake you are trying to breed, to see what might be occurring in the wild to trigger reproduction.

Light Cycles

Many pythons are tropical snakes and don't see a wide variation in day length from winter to fall. Some breeders pay little attention to this aspect, keeping their snakes on a 12-on, 12-off light cycle. Other breeders will shorten the winter light cycle down to 8 or 10 hours of daylight, even though most of them admit that temperature manipulation seems to be more important. It is very easy to adjust the light cycle and we have always felt it was helpful to induce breeding. If you use a timer on your cage lights, you can simply shorten the day length by five minutes a day or 30 minutes a week

Ball pythons (Python regius) *may have gold or black (seen here) vertebral stripes.*

A male will drag his body across the female's and nudge her with his chin to elicit breeding behavior.

until the winter solstice, and then reverse the process, lengthening the day to 15 hours or whatever your day length might be. If this seems to be a lot of trouble, use a reverse photoelectric cell that turns the lights on as the day breaks, and off again at sunset.

Temperature Cycles
Temperature fluctuations seem to be the most important cue in inducing python breeding.

Cool evening temperature. Most breeders will cycle their pythons at the beginning of the breeding season by dropping the evening temperature to around 70°F (21°C) for a period of six to eight hours, and then raising the daytime temperature back to normal levels. This is done for about a month prior to introducing the sexes to each other, and for about a month afterward. At the end of this time, temperatures should be returned to their normal day and night levels.

The size and shape of the everted hemipenes is species-specific.

Copulation

Adding the Male
Once your snakes are in good health, with good but not heavy body weight, and you've cycled them to ready them for breeding, you can introduce the male into the female's cage. Stimulated by the scent of a new, unfamiliar snake, both snakes should display immediate interest and begin to explore each other.

Courtship
Copulation often occurs almost immediately, but it usually is preceded by a certain amount of courtship with the male following the female around the cage and then crawling over her. Both snakes will be flicking their tongues as they take in what must be a powerful series of pheromone scents. Just prior to copulation, the male's spurs are often used to stimulate the female's cloacal area.

Sperm Viability
Sometimes copulation will occur at night and may not be observed, but when you do see copulation, it usually lasts for an hour or so. This is an ideal chance to check the male's sperm for viability. At the time the pair separates, enough sperm is normally dropped onto the floor of the cage to enable you to retrieve a sample and look at it under a microscope. The individual sperm should be numerous, active, and appear uniformly shaped.

Using Two Males
You can stimulate copulation in your snakes by using two males. Males are usually aggressive toward each other at this time of the year and will display some kind of combat behavior. The safe way to exploit this behavior is to place one male in the female's cage, let him crawl around for a few minutes, and then remove him. Immediately

introduce another male into the female's cage, while the scent of the first male is still present. Some breeders will actually introduce two males to one female at the same time, allow combat behavior to begin, and then remove one male. If you try this, remember that males in combat behavior are apt to bite—quite fiercely—anything within reach.

Caution: Do not put together two male green tree pythons or two male reticulated pythons because of the severe, and often immediate, damage they do to each other by inflicting deep bites. Both species have specialized cutting or piercing teeth (see the species accounts for details), which are highly effective on their prey, each other, or a perceived enemy.

Gravid Females

Is She?

There are a number of indicators that indicate that a female is gravid. Shortly after copulation you may notice a mid-body bulge in your female. This will appear as a distinct and noticeable swelling, as though a meal has just been eaten, but will disappear within 24 to 48 hours. Radiographs have shown that these are the ova changing position in the female's body, moving forward from the ovaries to the oviducts, where they will be fertilized by the waiting sperm.

Development of the Eggs

As the eggs develop, some of the female's fat reserves will be used up and the back third of her body will become swollen, developing a pear-shaped appearance. At this stage, many females will go off feed as the body becomes filled with enlarging eggs. Regular basking behavior will usually be observed, often with the female turning the back half of her body upside down as she basks.

The gravid python will shed just about one month prior to egg deposition.

The Hot Spot

It is extremely important to provide a basking area for the female during the period in which she is carrying eggs. Gravid females will regularly bask at a heat source and will provide some interesting behavior for you to observe as they thermoregulate their bodies, moving to, then away, from the heat source.

Shedding before Laying

Most females will undergo a pre-laying shed, which occurs about a month prior to egg laying. This shedding is a useful tool in letting you know when to expect—and watch out for—egg laying. It gives you a chance to prepare the egg deposition site, acquire or build an incubator, and make sure you have food to offer the female once she has laid her eggs.

When you place an egg deposition box in the female's enclosure, she will begin to explore it.

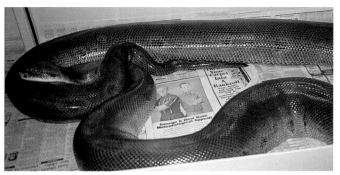

The ovulating python (here a green phase Burmese python, Python molurus bivittatus), *displays a distinct midbody swelling (just to the right of the uppermost length of the snake) after a successful breeding.*

Nesting Sites

Provide the Site

It is always a good idea to provide some kind of shelter supplied with moistened sphagnum moss as a nest site for your gravid female. There have been some observations that gravid female pythons that lack egg deposition sites actually will retain the eggs, or, as in the case of the green tree python, simply let the eggs fall to the cage bottom.

With smaller species, a plastic box with an entry hole will suffice. With the giant pythons it may not be feasible to build a covered box, but you can provide a large deep tray of moistened medium, or simply pile the dampened sphagnum on the floor of the cage. The female snake will generally move the sphagnum aside to lay her eggs, but you can nestle the sphagnum around her to provide humidity for the eggs.

Place the Site

Where you place the egg deposition box inside your cage depends on the kind of python you are keeping. With arboreal species such as the green tree python, the box should be hung on the wall of the cage; gravid green tree pythons do not descend to the cage floor for egg deposition. Terrestrial species need a box on the bottom of the cage.

Once you've placed the egg deposition box within the cage, the gravid female should begin exploring it, crawling into it and out again, and smelling it thoroughly with her tongue. As her due date approaches, she will spend more and more time within the box, often with just the tip of her nose showing. Do not expect her to be friendly at this time. Check her daily, especially as the one-month-after-her-last-shed date approaches. You'll need to decide if you'd like to incubate the eggs, or if you'd like the female to do the incubation—if she will. Once she has laid her eggs, the next step is up to you.

Laying the Eggs

Once the female has begun to lay her eggs, do not disturb her until she has completed the process; for most pythons, this will take about six to ten hours. When she is done, you have just a few hours to remove them for incubation before they begin to stick together in a more or less coherent mass.

Caution: If a gravid female sheds, and if after four weeks she hasn't laid

Heavily gravid pythons often lie upside down, "sunning" their bellies.

44

her eggs, consult your veterinarian. The eggs may need to be surgically excised, and unfortunately, these eggs will not hatch.

Removing the Eggs

For smaller species, you can wear a pair of leather gloves to protect your hands as you uncoil the female from around her eggs, pick up the eggs, and nestle them singly in the incubation sphagnum or vermiculite. Use a pencil to mark an X on the upper side of the eggs, so you can keep this side up.

For the larger species, such as the Burmese or reticulated pythons, the simplest way to remove the eggs is to throw a blanket completely over the snake, then reach in under the front edge of the blanket, lift the coils, and push them backwards over and beyond the eggs. Pick up the eggs, mark the top side with a penciled X, and put them in the incubator. As you handle each egg, look for any that are smaller than the rest, yellowish, or misshapen. These are infertile and should be discarded. If the eggs have dried into one contiguous pile, try to gently separate them. If they stick together too firmly to take apart, remove the pile intact and place the eggs into the incubator. As they near their hatching date, the eggs tend to become less adhesive.

Using Two People

If the female has coiled around her eggs, removing the eggs is easier if there are two people involved. The first person cups his or her hands around the female, keeping her head against her coils, and begins to lift her, while the second person works from the side and gently removes the eggs. When you actually begin to touch the eggs, be certain to keep the same side up, to prevent any possible shifting of the embryo in relationship to the air pocket inside the egg.

Removing the eggs from an incubating female can be done by one person, but would be easier for two people. The female is usually very protective of her eggs.

Taking the eggs singlehandedly is a bit ticklish, because the female tends to coil around, on top of, and in between the eggs on the edge of the clutch. If she shifts suddenly in response to your hands, she may crush some of her eggs, and the eggs may shift from their original this-side-up position. If both of your hands are busy trying to pin the female and remove eggs at the same time, your face is left unprotected and uncomfortably close to the female.

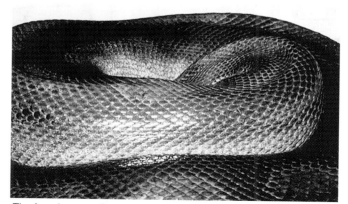

The female green Burmese python inspects the eggs she is incubating, and uses her tongue to check temperature levels. If the temperature inside her coils is too cool, she will increase her shivering rate.

HOW-TO:
Sexing Your Snake

Make certain that you have both sexes of your python species. If these are snakes that you purchased as babies and raised, they should have been sexed as soon as you received them so any errors could be addressed with your supplier.

If you're not certain you have both sexes, there are three ways to find out:

Popping

Most hatchling pythons can be sexed by popping or manually everting the hemipenes. This is done just after hatching or within a few days of hatching, while the snake itself is still very pliable. Grasp the hatchling by the rear of the body, turning the snake over, and place your thumb on the underside of the tail, about ½ inch (13 mm) behind the cloaca. Apply gentle but firm pressure, and roll your thumb all the way to the cloacal opening. If the hatchling is a male, the hemipenes should evert, appearing as short, red stubs. If no hemipenes appear, the snake is a female.

Warning: There are a few points to remember before you try manual eversion. Do not use this technique on a hatchling that is cloudy and about to shed, as the skin can easily be torn at this time. Do not use this technique on hatchling green tree pythons, where it will cause tail kinking problems. Don't use this technique on snakes that are older than a few days, because

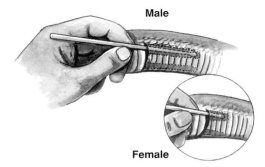

Male

Female

Step 1—Gently insert the blunt probe into one of two small openings in the base of the tail, until resistance is felt. Mark the point of deepest penetration with your thumbnail before extracting the probe.

Step 2—Hold the probe against the tail, with your thumbnail again at the vent, to determine the depth probed in terms of subcaudal scales. Average probe depth will be 2 to 5 scales for females and 7 to 12 scales for males.

Probes can be used to help sex a python.

the pressure you apply may cause permanent tail kinking and/or damage the hemipenes.

Probing

For these older snakes, you'll need to probe the snake to determine the length of the hemipenes (males) or the musk glands (females). In this process, a lubricated shaft of the proper dimension (the probe) is inserted into the cloacal opening of the snake. The male's hemipenes are longer than the female's musk glands, and so the depth to which the

probe can be inserted reveals the snake's sex.

To probe a snake, hold the tail of the snake in one hand, and turn it underside-up. The probe (lubricated with K-Y Jelly or Vaseline) is inserted into the cloacal opening of the snake, in the direction of the tail. The depth is measured by counting the number of subcaudal scales. For the females, the probe can generally be inserted to the depth of two to four subcaudal scales. A probe inserted into a male snake, on the other hand, can be inserted the total length of the hemipenis, generally to a depth of eight to fifteen subcaudal scales.

Probing works on all pythons except for those types that have short tails. For pythons like the ball pythons and the blood pythons, the hemipenes and the musk gland are about the same length, and probing is inconclusive. (Sexing these pythons is very much an educated guess, based on general appearance and width of the tail.)

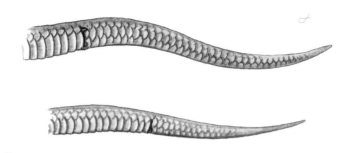

Compare tail length and width to differentiate between male and female snakes.

Appearance

It is also possible to sex your snakes by looking at the tail; the male has a wider, longer tail than the female. Males usually have longer spurs than the females; these are located outside the cloaca and are very obvious. If the female does have spurs, they are very tiny. Obviously, being able to make these comparisons requires that you have at least two snakes—and preferably of the opposite sex—to be able to see what "wider" means or what "longer spurs" look like.

Hatchlings of the green and labyrinth phases of the Burmese python are seen here.

Retained Eggs

Once the female has laid her eggs, check to make sure she hasn't retained any. These generally appear as egg-sized lumps in the lower half of the body. You can sometimes feel them by gently running her body through your hand.

Once costing several thousand dollars each, hatchling albino Burmese pythons can now occasionally be purchased for less than $100.

If you discover retained eggs, wait a few weeks to see if she will pass the eggs on her own. Retained eggs are rarely viable, and if fully developed, cannot be resorbed by the female. Your veterinarian may use an injection of oxytocin, a hormone that stimulates egg laying, or opt for surgical intervention.

Brooding Behavior

After egg laying, it is important to get the female to begin feeding again. Sometimes she will still exhibit brooding behavior, remaining coiled in her egg deposition box and striking at any interloper, even though the eggs have been removed. Brooding females (or females that think they are brooding) do not feed, so you need to change this behavior.

Alter the Site

At the very least, remove the egg-laying box, or better still, move the female to another cage. Provide her with a hiding area but not, of course, a brooding box. If you pass by the cage and see the female has resumed her brooding position, remove her from the cage and handle her for a few minutes. Carry her around your home or simply support her body in your arms for a while, or even place her in a clean muslin snakebag for an hour or so.

Usually a few days of special attention will stop the brooding behavior. Watch her carefully during this time and treat her immediately at the first sign of illness.

Genetics

With the wide variety of aberrant colors and patterns now available in captive-bred pythons, it is useful to know something about how to breed for some of these traits. It is sometimes possible to combine different traits with one another, such as mixing

This baby ball python is axanthic, which means it lacks yellow pigment.

color and pattern defects together in order to create a new pattern or color variation. Some people will occasionally try to create a new-appearing snake by hybridizing two closely related species, but this is not recommended. These "mutts" have appeared on the market, but have been avoided by the majority of collectors simply because these snakes are a dead-end.

When you see a pattern or color variation in a snake, your first question should be "Is this genetic?" and the second, "Can it be repeated?" Many color and pattern variations are genetic, but some variations such as striping can also be caused by external factors during incubation, such as low incubation temperature.

The only way to know for sure is to breed for the trait you are seeking. This may take two generations to appear, if the trait you are interested in is recessive.

Working with Color

In reptiles, colors in the skin are produced by three types of pigment cells, called *melanophores* (for brown and black), *xanthophores* (for red and yellow), and *iridophores* (which contain reflective minerals that result in khaki, blue, green, and red hues). Each type of color cell is in a specific layer within the dermis or skin.

Each color is determined by two genes, one dominant and the other recessive. Each snake carries two genes for each color or pattern. A snake with normal coloration has at least one dominant gene for normal coloration. If the second gene is for normal coloration, the snake can only pass on dominant genes for normal coloration.

However, if a snake has one dominant gene for normal coloration and a recessive gene for albinism (is *heterozygous* for albinism), breeding that snake with an albino (two recessive genes for albinism or *homozygous* for albinism) results in a split litter: Half of the young will appear normal, but bear one gene for normal coloration (the dominant gene) and the second gene for albinism (the recessive gene). These are heterozygous for albinism. The other half of the litter, the albinos, will have two recessive genes for albinism, and will be homozygous for albinism.

Four Pigments

When you're dealing with four pigments, color variations and permutations seem pretty infinite. The term *albino* is used to indicate the absence of pigment, not necessarily black pigment. You can have a "red" albino, missing the black and yellow pigment, a "black" albino, missing the red and yellow pigment, a "white" albino, missing red, black, and yellow pigments, or a "yellow" albino, missing the red and black pigments.

There is no way to look at a snake of normal coloration and determine if it is heterozygous or homozygous; you have to know what the parents were.

Combining Coloration and Striping

When you combine two unrelated recessive genes such as coloration (we'll use albinism as an example) and striping, the computations get a bit more complicated, but are still workable. The first clutch from this cross will be all normal babies, but double heterozygous, meaning carrying both recessive genes that are masked by the dominant gene. If you raise these babies up and breed a pair of them to each other, you'll get a

mixed bag in terms of appearance and genetics. The young of this cross will be typically three albino/normal patterned babies, three striped babies, nine normal color/normal patterned, three normal color/striped and one albino-striped baby, the one you were trying to create. Once you get this first striped albino you can breed it in the same way as your original albino, to create a new line of snakes.

Those other babies in the litter can be sold. Pythons bearing recessive genes for desired colors or patterns are generally valued more than the normally colored, normally patterned babies.

As you will see, when trying to produce new colors or patterns, it is sometimes necessary to inbreed brother to sister or mother to son. This first generation inbreeding is usually not harmful, but inbreeding should not be carried beyond this point. You should always keep a written record of your bloodlines and make every effort to breed unrelated snakes.

Breeding for Unusual Mixes

Breeding for special colors and patterns is still in its infancy, with a great deal of time, effort, and money being expended simply to discover the parameters of what breeds true and what doesn't. If a trait is thought to be recessive, at best the breeder needs to breed and raise up three generations of snakes before a possible variant can be considered predictable. The chart below will show you some of the current variations for Burmese pythons, and indicate some possible combinations.

Burmese Python	Coloration
Amelanistic Albino	
bred with:	
Amelanistic Albino	Young: orange, yellow and white; Adults: bright lemon and white.
Green	Young: bright orange and white with deeper orange stripe down back; Adults: yellow with indistinct pattern.
Labyrinth	Mazelike pattern of orange on pinky-lavender background.
Granite	Unknown.
Green	
bred with:	
Amelanistic Albino	Young: bright orange and white with deeper orange stripe down back; Adults: yellow with indistinct pattern.
Green	Young: khaki dorsally, silver ventrally with broken line of chocolate down the back.
Labyrinth	Unknown.
Granite	Unknown.
Labyrinth	
bred with:	
Amelanistic Albino	Mazelike pattern of orange on pinky-lavender background.
Green	Unknown.
Labyrinth	Mazelike pattern of gold on dark brown. background.
Granite	Unknown.
Granite	
bred with:	
Amelanistic Albino	Unknown.
Green	Unknown.
Labyrinth	Unknown.
Granite	Small brown reticulations on yellow background; pale, unmarked head, pale venter.

Incubation

For anyone attempting to breed pythons, an incubator is a crucial piece of equipment. Even if you chose to let the female incubate her eggs, an incubator "on standby" gives you the option of taking over the incubation process if something goes wrong. The actual acquisition of an incubator is easy; one can be purchased, ready-made, or you can make a perfectly serviceable unit from easily obtainable hardware materials (see How To Make an Incubator for details).

Commercial Incubators

These range in price from about $60 for a simple box-design model to $4,000 for a sophisticated unit that will monitor heat, humidity, and carbon dioxide levels. Most of the major reptile trade magazines have ads each month for commercial incubators. If you prefer to deal locally, your local reptile/pet shop should be able to help you.

There are a few components involved with any incubator:

1. A fan to circulate the air in the incubator and thus keep the humidity and temperatures even. If you're dealing with the smaller species of python, with fewer and smaller eggs, the lack of a fan is not as critical. But if you're breeding a large python, like the reticulated, the 60+ eggs produced take up quite a bit of space. You'll need a larger incubator, and a continuously operating fan does help keep moisture and heat levels evenly distributed.

2. Two thermostats, wired in line with each other. If one fails, the second one can take over. For a home-made incubator, the wafer thermostats commonly used cost about $10 each, so the outlay for this type of security is modest.

3. A heat source. Commercial units may use a shielded heating coil; homemade incubators utilize a heat tape. These are available from gardening or hardware stores, and come in different wattages. We have found that a tape that uses 250–300 watts is large enough for an incubator about 4 feet (1.2 m) square.

4. A ventilated shelving system. Shelves in the incubator should be made of screen or wire to permit an easy flow of air throughout the unit.

Letting the Female Incubate Her Eggs

In most cases, you'll want to remove freshly laid eggs from the female

A commercial incubation unit will monitor and adjust temperature and humidity levels. No incubation medium is needed.

python and place them in an incubator, but there may be time when it is easier or more convenient to allow the female to incubate her own eggs.

Depending on where you live, you may need to provide additional heat for the female python. Only a few species utilize quivering to generate heat for the eggs, so additional heat may be necessary (this isn't always true in warm areas like Florida). Ideally, for the female to successfully incubate her eggs, the cage temperature needs to be from 86 to 90°F (30–32.2°C) for northern climates to 82 to 85°F (27.8–29.4°C) in southern climates. In the southern states (like Florida), where winter months are significantly warmer, this means that air conditioning may be needed to cool the room/caging system to 82 to 85°F.

If the cage is too warm, the female may loosen her coils (or, in a worst-case scenario, leave the eggs), allowing the eggs to desiccate. Even the loosening of the coils will permit the uppermost and outermost eggs to dry out.

There are cases of the female leaving the eggs to bask and warm her body and then returning to coil around the eggs. Some female pythons will feed during the maternal incubation period, although most of them fast.

The female will drink water during incubation, either by leaving the eggs and seeking out her water dish or by drinking from her coils if misted. The egg deposition box, with its layer of damp sphagnum, will help maintain the proper level of humidity, but you'll need to monitor the dampness of the sphagnum during the incubation period. If the female enters her drinking pool and then returns immediately to coil around her eggs, check the moisture level of the incubating medium. She may be trying to remoisten her eggs by carrying moisture on her body surface. If needed, use a water spritzer to add moisture to the eggs.

Ball pythons can either be allowed to incubate their own eggs or the eggs can be removed and incubated artificially. This clutch is in a net hammock.

Other than the necessary checks to determine moisture and temperature levels, try to disturb your incubating female as little as possible.

Patterned when young but patternless when adult, the "green" phase is only one of several selectively bred colors of the Burmese python (Python molurus bivittatus).

HOW-TO:
Making Your Own Incubator

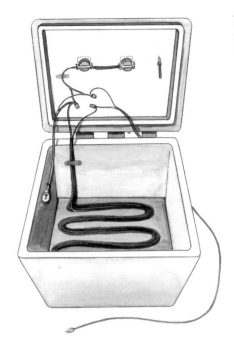

A large styrofoam cooler, wafer thermostat, and heat tape can be used to build a very serviceable incubator.

Materials Needed for One Incubator

• 1 wafer thermostat/heater (obtainable from feed stores; these are commonly used in incubators for chicks)
• 1 thermometer
• 1 heat tape (obtained from hardware or garden stores)
• 1 styrofoam cooler (one with thick sides—a fish shipping box is ideal)
• 1 electric cord with plug

Directions

1. Poke a hole through the lid of the styrofoam cooler, and suspend the thermostat/heater from the inside. Add another hole for a thermometer so you can check the inside temperature without opening the top. If there's no flange on the thermometer to keep it from slipping through the hole in the lid, use a rubber band wound several times around the thermometer to form a flange.

2. Transverse the bottom of the cooler with the heat tape and wire the tape to the thermostat, and the electric cord to the thermostat.

3. Put the lid on the cooler, and plug in the thermostat/heater. Wait half an hour, then check the temperature. Adjust the thermostat/heater until the temperature inside the incubator is about 80 to 86°F (27–30°C) (see the species accounts beginning on page 56 so you'll know what temperature to use). The L-pin "han-

dle" on the top of the thermostat is the rheostat.

4. Once you have the temperature regulated, put the container of eggs inside the incubator and close the lid.

5. Check the temperature daily and add a little water to the incubating medium as needed. The preferred humidity is 100%, which can be accomplished by keeping the hatching medium of peat and soil damp to the touch but too dry to squeeze out any water by hand.

Artificial Incubation

If your female is laying her eggs, or if you've decided to remove the eggs being cared for by an incubating python,

get your incubator ready. Turn it on and let it warm up, to 88 to 90°F (31.1–32.2°C). Prepare a series of egg "storage" boxes with incubation medium, and let them warm up in the incubator.

Boxes to Use

The boxes used to house the eggs during incubation are generally appropriately sized plastic boxes with ventilation holes and a solid lid. Incubation material can be moistened perlite, sphagnum, peat moss, or vermiculite. To moisten the material, simply add water, stir to mix, then remove handfuls and squeeze until you can't squeeze any more water out. The medium should be damp enough to hold its shape when squeezed.

Removing the Eggs

If you decide to remove the eggs from an incubating female, she will probably not offer to bite during this process, but she may push at you or butt you with her coils, and this can be quite startling. Mark each egg with a penciled X to indicate the upward side as the egg was laid.

Once you have removed the eggs, look for any that are small or misshapen and discard them. If you are unsure if some eggs are bad, go ahead and set up the clutch in incubation. Your nose will tell you in about ten days if the eggs are fertile or not.

Placing the Eggs in the Incubator

Nestle the eggs in the incubation medium, marked side up. Check the temperature daily and keep the incubation medium moist. The hatching medium of peat and soil should be damp to the touch but too dry to squeeze out any water when squeezed by your hand.

Determining Fertility

How do you know if the eggs are fertile? By the end of the first week, those eggs that are not fertile will turn yellow, harden, and begin to collapse. Those that are fertile will remain white and turgid to the touch. Infertile eggs may mold, but this is seldom transferred to healthy eggs.

Stages of Incubating

During the first six to eight weeks of incubation the eggs should gradually swell as they develop. If during this time the eggs are beginning to indent, it means they are not getting enough moisture and you need to check the level of humidity.

In the final week of incubation, most eggs will begin to indent. This is normal, but at this time it is extremely important for the eggs to have adequate ventilation in the incubator.

There are tiny snakes inside those eggs, and they now need more oxygen than before.

The Babies

At the end of the incubation period—which may be as little as two weeks for some species but is usually 60–70 days—the baby pythons will cut a slit in their egg with the egg tooth on the tip of their snout.

The babies do not seem eager to leave the egg. They will cut a slit, look out, and decide to stay inside the egg for a while longer, perhaps as long as a day and a half. Those that leave the egg can be removed to other terrariums or plastic shoe boxes and offered food, a sunning spot, and water. They should shed within a few days.

Caution: Don't help. Although this may try your patience, you cannot help the babies out of their eggs. For unhatched eggs, two days after the rest of the other eggs hatch, you *can* cut a tiny wedge-shaped window into the egg. Lift the wedge gently and peer inside. If a bright-eyed baby snake peers back, replace the egg in the incubator and hope the baby snake gets the hint. If the baby snake inside is dead, there is nothing you can do except dispose of the egg. Very few clutches have a 100 percent hatch rate.

Extras

Once your baby pythons have shed and are eating on their own, you may want to dispose of some. Check with your local herpetological society. Many of them allow captive-bred babies to be sold at their monthly meetings or through their newsletter. If you want to sell entire clutches of babies, contact the dealers who advertise in the national reptile magazines. There are also regional reptile expositions where breeders buy tablespace and sell their captive-born progeny.

Species Accounts

Children's Python Complex (*Antaresia* spp.)

Most hobbyists remember the Children's python as *Liasis childreni*, an Australian snake of several variably colored subspecies. *L. childreni* no longer exists, due to revisionist work done by Arnold Kluge, a taxonomist from the University of Michigan (Ann Arbor). Kluge's careful scrutiny and subsequent classification revision of reptiles has many of us laboriously inking in new names in our field guides of several countries.

Our old friend, *childreni*, has been divided into four new species. All are tidily included in *Antaresia*, named for Antares, the brightest star in the skies of the Southern Hemisphere.

Antaresia are all brown pythons, patterned with blotches, divided by geographic distribution and other characteristics. They range in size

The small and easily-handled, spotted python (Antaresia maculosa) *is the most common member of the Children's python complex now in herpetoculture.*

from 18 to 23 inches (46–58 cm) (the anthill python) to 69 inches (175 cm) (the spotted python).

Typically, members of *Antaresia* have a thermosensory pit in the first scale of the upper labials, and four to six thermosensory pits in the posterior lower labials. As a group, they have more teeth than most pythons. Their basic food item in the wild is lizards.

The easiest way to tell the four species apart used to be by geographic origin, but that has become almost impossible with "mutts" from captive-breeding programs, lost collecting data, and over-zealous salesmanship. Determining which species is which in captivity can take on the aspect of a major challenge.

Spotted Python (*Antaresia maculosa*)

This is the most popular *Antaresia* species in American, Australian, and European collections. At least four generations of what people *used* to think were Children's pythons have been bred in the United States. Some lineages may be traceable back to a pair imported from Cape York Peninsula of northeastern Queensland, Australia. These descendants can be distinguished by their large size and pale yellow bellies.

Appearance: The pale to reddish dorsum of *A. maculosa* is marked with dark blotches. The dark blotches may join to form larger blotches or wavy lines along part of the dorsal surface. Unlike other members of *Antaresia*, the blotches remain distinct and sharply defined as the snake matures.

Size: Adults are 43 to 47 inches (110–120 cm) and, rarely, to 65 inches (170 cm).

Range: Eastern and northeastern Australia

Habitat: Woodland, forest, and semiarid areas.

Breeding: This popular python breeds readily in captivity. Females lay large eggs but only two to twelve per clutch. Eggs hatch about two months after incubation at 85 to 90°F (29–33°C). The hatchlings feed on pinkies (newborn mice).

Care Notes: As with other examples of *Antaresia*, the blotched python lives well in pairs, trios, or as two pairs. The males do not seem to be territorial. Although this is the largest of the genus, it is not a big python, and its good disposition and ready breeding account for its popularity.

Although of variable color, the small and pretty Children's python (Antaresia childreni) often has rather poorly defined, reddish dark spots against a tan or blonde background.

Children's Python (*Antaresia childreni*)

In 1842 John Edward Gray, Keeper of the Zoological Collection at the British Museum, came across a small, nondescript preserved snake from Australia in the collection of the museum. He named the snake *Liasis childreni*, the specific name in honor of his predecessor, John G. Children. The name stuck, but unfortunately we applied it to the wrong snake. Although the name is the same as what we used to call the Children's python, *that* Children's python and *this* Children's python are entirely separate creatures (of course this is confusing—taxonomy is a very inexact science).

The original-but-heretofore-unrecognized Children's python is *Antaresia childreni*, one of the smallest pythons in the world. For many hobbyists, it is the ultimate python, very much a python yet gentle and easily kept in a 20-gallon-sized (76 L) tank.

Appearance: Brown splotches dot the red, reddish-brown, or yellow dorsum of this gentle snake. Markings tend to blend into the background coloration by three to six years of age. Along the dorsolateral edge, just above the belly scutes, two lines of dark markings parallel each other to create a paler "stripe" that extends for the first third to half the length of the body. A purple iridescence is evident along the curves of the coils in adults. The underside is paler and unmarked. The tongue is red with gray tips.

Size: Adult, just over 3 feet (1 m); one of the largest recorded was just over 44 inches (99 cm).

Range: North central coastal areas of Australia.

Habitat: Dry woodland, rocky aridlands, and forested areas; coastal plains, grass savannas, along river edges and in large termite mounds. This species is essentially nocturnal. It can be found in caves, where it waits, on a rocky ledge or hanging from a crevice, for its bat prey. It can constrict and eat a bat while hanging from its tail tip.

Breeding: If males are placed together during the fall breeding season, they will engage in wrestling and biting male combat behavior, but *childreni* breed so readily that this type of stimulus is not necessary. Male-female pairs can either be kept together year-round, or maintained separately and placed together in the fall.

Food for both the males and female is withheld beginning in the late fall, and the cage temperature reduced to 67 to 73°F (20–23°C). Daylight hours are shortened to eight to nine hours. A warm spot (heat tape, heating pad, or spot light) may or may not be offered (we like to err on the side of caution, and always offer a warm spot) during this cooling period.

Childreni will copulate repeatedly until early spring. Ovulation indicates that the female in question will soon be gravid, and the pairs should be separated at this time. The gravid females will utilize nest boxes filled with damp sphagnum.

The large-blotched python (Antaresia stimsoni) *is still uncommon in herpetoculture, but is growing in popularity.*

The gravid females shed 19 days after ovulation, and lay their eggs 23 days after shedding. The usual time for egg deposition is March to May.

Females lay small numbers (2 to 12) of rather large eggs. The females will coil about their eggs, but no thermoregulatory shivering takes place. The eggs will stick to each other and become less adherent as the hatching date approaches. Incubation generally takes 60 days at 85 to 90°F (29–33°C).

The first shed occurs a week or two after hatching. Neonates usually feed on pink mice, two to six weeks after shedding. Some hatchlings need to be tempted by scenting the pinky with a lizard. You can create a scenting gruel by chopping up a skink tail and boiling it in a cup of water. This gruel can be used to dip-scent lots of mice, and is an efficient way to "stretch" a skink tail. If you only have a few snakes, you can freeze the gruel in an ice cube tray, and then empty the cubes into a plastic bag kept in your freezer. You can then thaw a cube every time you need to scent food. Be very sure to label the bag.

Care Notes: A pair of this gentle python can be kept in a 20- to 30-gallon (76–114 L) terrarium. They feed primarily on newborn rats or on mice; young snakes in the wild add frogs and lizards to their diet. Their good disposition, small size, easy adaptability to captivity, and mouse diet make these pythons a good pet choice.

Large-blotched Python (*Antaresia stimsoni*)

The large-blotched python, along with the white-lipped python (*Leiopython albertisii*), bears the distinction of having the most teeth— 150—of any python species. This snake with the big dorsal blotches has the widest geographical range in Australia of all the Australian pythons, and its small size has made it a high priority in captive-breeding programs. The large-blotched python may seem nippy at first, but settles down with repeated and consistent handling.

Appearance: Large maroon blotches adorn this small python. The base color of the snake is yellow, but the size and close positioning of the blotches make the snake appear darker. Some examples look superficially like a North American chain kingsnake in pattern and color, while others look like reticulate giraffes. Overall, there is an enormous geographic range of size, pattern, and color with the Stimson's pythons. We can expect to see some taxonomic splitting of this species as time goes on.

Both the large-blotched and the Children's pythons can be readily distinguished from other small pythons (especially the small-blotched python) by the presence of a distinctive pale lateral line, bordered top and bottom by darker blotches, extending from the neck along the first third to half the length of the body.

Large-blotched pythons can be distinguished from Children's pythons by their longer snout and larger eyes.

Size: From 35 to 39 inches (90–100 cm).

Range: Large-blotched pythons have a huge range, extending from extreme western throughout central Australia. Their exact distribution over this range has not yet been determined, because this is an area the size of the United States.

Habitat: Large-blotched pythons are found in very arid conditions, on rocky ridges and hillsides, grasslands, and spinifex scrublands. They have been found in termite mounds and caves with resident bat populations, areas that would retain some measure of humidity. The larger eyes may

indicate nocturnal activity patterns, a typical behavioral adaptation to desert environments.

Breeding and Care Notes: Although a few examples of Stimson's python are found in captivity in Australia, they are relatively new in captivity in the United States. The breeding regimen for these snakes would be much the same as for the other species of *Antaresia*, with reduction of cage temperature and placing the sexes together in the late fall, copulation from December through March, and egg deposition in April to May. Incubation is about 52 days.

Anthill Python
Antaresia perthensis

This small python was formerly known as the Perth python. It lives in termite mounds, which are called anthills in Australia. It feeds primarily on lizards.

Appearance: Yellowish to reddish with poorly defined blotching. In some examples the blotching may appear as paired markings on each side of the dorsum, but this is not a consistent characteristic. As the snake ages, the blotching becomes less and less distinct. Older animals may appear unicolored. The snout is blunt and rounded.

Size: Small, reaching 18 to 23 inches (48–56 cm) as an adult. An occasional "sumo" specimen may reach 27 inches (69 cm).

Range: Pilbara and the adjacent rocky territories in northwest Australia. The specific name, *perthensis*, was chosen because the type specimen was mistakenly identified as being from Perth. In reality, these snakes occur nowhere near Perth, but changing the specific name is not an option.

Habitat: Arid areas in the northwestern section of western Australia.

Breeding: In the wild, this small python not only lives in termitaria but lays its eggs there as well. Captive

The large Papuan python (Apodora papuana) *has interestingly sculptured head scales.*

perthensis lay few (two to five) eggs, and the female coils around the clutch. No thermoregulatory shivering has been noted. Incubation at 85 to 87°F (29–31°C) lasts for 45 to 60 days before hatchlings emerge. The neonates are small, about 7.5 inches (190 cm), and evidently feed on small skinks and other lizards.

Care Notes: This small python is extremely hardy. It adapts well to captivity and breeds readily. Despite the rarity of the snake in captivity, this small-sized python seems to be a hardy snake under good captive conditions.

Papuan Python
(*Apodora papuanus*)

The Papuan python was a member of *Liasis*, but the 1993 reclassification by Arnold Kluge created this monotypic genus for this nonconforming snake.

Appearance: This is an olive-gray to olive-brown python, paler ventrally, with heat-sensitive pits along the upper labials and posterior lower labials. The scales are smooth. The black interstitial skin imparts a reticulated effect to the dorsum, and the snake may look vaguely spotted with black where the dorsum is scarred. This is a heavily built python with a shortened head.

Size: Adults may get up to 14 feet (4.27 m). Although this is not necessarily the longest New Guinea snake, it is the heaviest. Hatchlings are 20 inches (51 cm).

Origin: Western New Guinea, both in Papua and Irian Jaya.

Range/Habitat: Low monsoon forests, dry grassland, woodlands. Due to its size, this python is largely terrestrial. Adults are often killed on roadsides within their habitat.

Breeding: When males and females are introduced to each other during breeding season, antagonistic behavior may result, and the initial sparring should be monitored to assure that neither snake is badly damaged. Captive reproduction of this snake is limited, but it seems to be a late-summer breeder with ovulation and egg deposition in November. Eggs were incubated at 89 to 91°F (31–33.5°C) and hatching occurred after 82 to 93 days.

Care Notes: The Papuan python eats mammals, birds, and other snakes. In the wild, the adults can overpower and consume wallabies of 45 pounds (20 kg).

The young quite likely are at least partially arboreal and are opportunistic feeders on both warm- and cold-blooded prey. These pythons are fairly readily available on dealers' lists, but have limited popularity due to their adult size and readiness to bite.

Aspidites: The Black-Headed Python and the Woma

Black-Headed Python
(*Aspidites melanocephalus*)

The two species in the genus *Aspidites*, the black-headed *A. melanocephalus* and the non-black-headed *A. ramsayi*, are among the most primitive of pythons. Both species are very popular with herpetoculturists, but were, until recently, practically impossible to acquire. Now, however, both are rather readily available; it merely takes upwards of $5,000 to become an owner of a pair of either species.

Appearance: Black headed pythons are of variable ground color, but usually are prominently banded snakes. The mid-dorsal area is the darkest and the straw-yellow and reddish-brown bands are most prominent laterally. The belly is an unrelieved yellow.

Size: Although most are 5 to 7 feet (1.5–2.1 m) or smaller, black heads can approach 8 feet (2.4 m) in total length. They are moderately heavy-bodied and are powerful constrictors.

Habitat: The black-headed python ranges throughout the northern two-fifths of Australia. It usually shuns aridlands and deserts, preferring instead the moister coastal forests and woodlands.

Breeding: Because of a paucity of specimens, successful breeding programs with this interesting snake were late in coming to American hobbyists and even to zoos. Under the tutelage of James Murphy, Dallas was one of the first institutions to succeed with the species. Other zoos and several private herpetoculturists have now followed suit.

Even under captive conditions, this is a late maturing python. Sexual maturity may not be attained until five years of age or later. For inexplicable reasons, black-headed pythons are still more problematic than womas (see following description). Sustained courtship and breeding activities may still not result in eggs.

Greatest success has been reached when winter cooling and photoperiod adjustment have occurred. Combat, at times savage, has been reported between sexually active males. Some breeders feel that such stimulation may be an important factor in successful breedings.

In nature, the coveted aridland, black-headed python (Aspidites melanocephalus) *feeds largely on lizards and other snakes.*

In America, where seasons are reversed 180 degrees from those in Australia, black-headed pythons are winter breeders. Eggs are laid through the months of spring and hatching occurs some two to two and a half months following deposition. Small clutches (five to eight, rarely a few more) of large eggs are produced. Females often prepare depressions in the substrate for their clutch. Although they may remain with the clutch, they are not known to thermoregulate. Hatchlings are often 20 inches (51 cm) or more in length.

Care Notes: One of the most important facts to remember about this snake species is that it is cannibalistic! When you are dealing with a snake that costs in excess of $2,500, this can be critical information.

Black-headed pythons remain among the most expensive of the constricting snakes. Fortunately, they have also proven hardy and undemanding in captivity. They are primarily nocturnal, seeking seclusion during the hours of daylight.

Once among the rarest of pythons in herpetoculture, the hardy and beautiful woma (Aspidites ramsayi) *is now readily available, but expensive.*

Those that we have had have fed readily on laboratory rodents. In the wild they accept, besides rodents, suitably sized marsupials, ground-nesting birds, lizards, and other snakes, including venomous elapines.

Woma
(*Aspidites ramsayi*)

Twenty years ago womas were virtually unobtainable in the United States. Today there are dozens of breeders and the species, although still expensive at upwards of $4,000 a pair, is readily available.

Appearance: Variable shades of yellow to tan with prominent cross-bands of darker brown to almost black. These crossbands are narrower than the light bands, and may occasionally have a reddish cast. The ventral surface is paler than the dorsum. Juveniles can have patches of black on the snout, but the adults do not have black heads.

Size: Womas are commonly 5½ to 6 feet (1.68–1.8 m), but sometimes grow to eight feet (2.4 m).

Range/Habitat: Unlike its cousin the black-headed python, which avoids excessively dry areas, the woma is firmly associated with semi-arid to desert areas. It is found in a broad east-west band across most of interior Australia.

Breeding: The woma seems easier to breed in captivity than its close relative, the black-headed python. Dick Goergen, who has bred both of these snakes on a consistent basis, drops the nighttime temperatures of his womas to 60°F (16°C) during the winter cooling period. Daytime highs are 10 degrees or more higher. Egg clutch size is small, averaging four to ten eggs. Babies are 16 to 18 inches (41–46 cm).

Care Notes: This is a nocturnal snake, and one that prefers to stay on the ground. It may be found during the day in burrows of small mammals (one of its favored prey items), or in hollowed logs or inside hollowed trees. Food items include mammals, birds, lizards, and other snakes, including elapine (cobra allies of several types) species.

Womas are, by and large, calm and docile snakes. Once stimulated by fear or the scent of food, however, they have the habit of biting and being slow to let go. If you are bitten, give the snake time to make up its mind to turn loose.

Womas are expensive snakes, due to their limited availability. Since Australia forbade exportation of its wildlife in the late sixties and seventies, any examples of this snake currently available in the United States are derivatives of captive-breeding programs in zoos, European breeding programs, or smuggled. Keep in mind that some countries do not have reciprocal agreements with Australia to protect/forbid the importation of Australian wildlife. Once an animal has somehow left Australia, there are no restrictions involved in bringing that animal into that nonreciprocal country.

Bothrochilus Pythons

Bismarck Ringed Python (*Bothrochilus boa*)

Until 1993 this small python was a member of the water python group, *Liasis*. Kluge's modification of that genus recreated an earlier genus, *Bothrochilus*, and its single member, the Bismarck ringed python. These are mild-mannered, agreeable pythons of a very workable size. Like other water-dependent members of the group, fairly high humidity is needed in the adult's enclosure, in the incubator, and in the hatchling's shoeboxes or other housing.

Appearance: If young ringed pythons retained their clownlike colors and patterns into adulthood, this would be the world's favorite python, hands down. The hatchlings are bright orange, dotted intermittently with large black spots. The spots in many places are big enough to form bands that circle the entire body, and a green iridescent "glaze" can be seen in the bends of the coils.

In snakes from the western part of the range, after the first six months the base color changes from orange to olive green, and the black dots are less obvious. The mature snakes are still attractive but are essentially dark snakes with bands of orange indistinctly visible beneath the dark pigmentation. The venter is light yellow.

Snakes from the eastern part of the range (New Ireland Province) tend to retain the ringed or banded appearance, but it dulls.

Interesting enough, the coloration and pattern of the immature or ringed phase is much like the patterns and colors exhibited by elapine species found in the same area. Protective mimicry may be a factor for the bright coloring of the Bismarck ringed python.

Size: This medium-sized python may be from 3 to 6 feet (.95–1.73 m).

Range: Bismarck Islands, off the coast of Papua New Guinea.

Habitat: Forests, open land, cultivated areas. May be diurnal or nocturnal.

Breeding: These snakes are best sexed by probing, since there are no distinct external characteristics. Males probe from three to four times deeper than the females' probe depth of two to three scales. Separation of the sexes prior to breeding does not seem to be necessary, since breeding has occurred in communal setups. In those setups, however, each snake had a hide box, so you may want to incorporate more than one in your caging arrangements.

Beautiful in a variable pattern of olive and orange when young (above), the Bismarck ringed python, Bothrochilus boa, *dulls in color with age (below).*

63

Although not every breeder has found photoperiod manipulation necessary for breeding, the very successful Houston Zoo has used both photoperiod and temperature manipulation to induce breeding. Summertime day length is increased up to 14 hours, with daytime temperatures in the mid-80s°F (26–30°C) and mid-to-upper 70s°F (24–26°C) at night. As daylight hours are reduced (see page 26 for the reduction factors), incrementally reduce daytime and nighttime temperatures by 10 and 15°, respectively. After two months at the lowest level of light and heat, begin to increase both the temperature and day length incrementally to summertime levels.

The females generally breed from December to March, and will lay their clutches after about 60 days of gestation, in March through July. Eggs are laid at night or in the early morning. Artificial incubation at 90°F (33°C) will take about 60 days, with the young emerging in April through September.

Care Notes: These are easy pythons to keep in captivity. Primarily terrestrial, they don't need a lot of vertical cage space. Like the other water pythons of *Liasis*, they like water, and need a big dish for soaking. Most will have difficulty shedding if not permitted to soak and/or if their cage is too dry. The cage should have a hot spot.

These snakes like to have a hide box, and will use it especially if they are startled by something outside their cage or if they feel nervous. If startled when constricting or feeding, they will leave the food item and not return to it. Adults eat other snakes, small rats, or mice. Since these snakes have proportionately small heads for their size, they prefer these smaller prey items. Young or hatchlings may eat lizards and small frogs; those reluctant to take a pinkie may do so if the item is scented with a lizard or frog. Occasionally a hatchling may eat fish; two neonates at the Houston Zoo preferentially ate freshwater fish, including goldfish but you should be aware that many herpeticulturists do not advocate the sustained feeding of goldfish to any reptile.

West African Burrowing Python (*Calabaria reinhardtii*)

The burrowing python is a secretive snake that spends its time under leaf litter and other debris. When confronted with a potential enemy, the burrowing python hides its head inside its protectively coiled body and bobs its rounded tail by way of distraction.

This is another one of the pythons whose taxonomy and status within the python group has been altered by Arnold Kluge, who feels this snake is a boa. His view has not yet been accepted by other taxonomists.

Appearance: *Calabaria* has a gently rounded, enlarged rostral scale on its nose tip, to aid in nudging its way through bark litter or leaf debris. It may make its own burrows, or find and follow those made by small mammals, which also are its main prey item. The burrowing python's head is

Although small and secretive, the burrowing python (Calabaria reinhardtii) *makes a hardy and interesting pet.*

not distinct from its cylindrical body, and the body scales are smooth. Basic coloration is dark brown, with intermittent diffuse orange blotches.

Size: Adults measure 18 inches (45 cm), infrequently as large as 40 inches (101 cm); hatchlings are 10 to 12 inches (25–30 cm) in length.

Range: West Africa, particularly Liberia and the Cameroons.

Habitat: Soft, moist, sandy-to-organic soils of woodlands; rodent burrows.

Breeding: John Meltzer, who has had great success in breeding western hog-nosed snakes, has been successful in breeding burrowing pythons. Published notes indicate the female lays from one to three large, elongated eggs, which do best when incubated in a humid incubator. The young are not as shy as the adults, and can be kept individually in terraria with a newspaper substrate. There they will accept pink mice, and the keeper can track which snake has shed and/or fed and which has not.

High humidity is needed for the adults as well as for the babies.

Care Notes: These hardy pythons, although fairly secretive, live well in a 20-gallon-sized (76 L) terrarium with about 5 to 6 inches (13–15 cm) of occasionally dampened peat-topsoil mixture or cypress mulch. The substrate needs to be deep enough to permit burrowing, and the water dish needs to be untippable. Wild-caught captives seem to prefer small rats to mice, a preference seemingly not shared by captive-born young. They will pin their prey against the sides of the burrow rather than constricting it, an efficient way to immobilize prey in very cramped quarters.

White-Lipped Python
(*Leiopython albertisii*)

There are three different color phases of the white-lipped (formerly and incorrectly known as the D'Albertis) python. Adults are universally considered bad-tempered, but these are such attractive snakes that dedicated hobbyists or professional herpetoculturists cannot resist working with them. As a result, there are now some good techniques available for handling the adults and the young.

As with many other species of pythons, the captive-born young seem to adjust more easily than the adults to handling, but that may be because more keepers are willing to be bitten by a 2-foot (61 cm) snake than an 8-foot (244 cm) snake, and therefore handle the smaller snakes more. In all honesty, frequent and consistent handling is the key for gentling a white lip of any age, as discouraging as it may seem. Whenever the size of the snake does not preclude it, use a snake hook to lift the python, then transfer it to your hand. This tends to avoid the bite-first-and-then-look response to an encroaching human hand.

The neonates are nervous, jumpy snakes that need easily accessed hiding areas (a substrate of wood shavings will help provide them with the security of seclusion). Do not take their consistent efforts to bite you personally; it takes time for them to realize that their keeper is not a predator.

The white-lipped python (Leiopython albertisii) *is a slender, often bad-tempered snake of moderate size. Several color morphs are known.*

Appearance: The three forms of the white-lipped python are solid black with white lips; gray, usually with a darker head and dark-peppered cream-colored labials; and the typical form, which has a dark back, golden flanks, a black head and dark, spotted white lips. This last form almost seems to glow when seen in the woods or in its cage.

The variety in coloration may indicate a species complex, rather than a single species. All three forms have soft, smooth skin, and gray to gray-brown eyes. They have large heads with expanded temporal regions. The tongue is blue gray with reddish sides and tip.

Size: 7 to 8 feet (2.1–2.4 m); the black morphs reach 9 feet (2.7 m). Hatchlings are 15 inches (38 cm).

Origin: Northern islands of Torres Strait, off the northern coast of Australia; New Guinea, in elevations of less than 6,250 feet (1,250 m). An isolated population is found on the island of Mussau, on the tip of the Bismarck Archipelago.

Range/Habitat: The white-lipped python is another of the water-loving pythons, and is found in rain forests, swamps, and grasslands, near water. Nocturnal, it may be seen on roadsides, especially after rain.

Breeding: Some breeders have found the white-lipped python needs large diurnal temperature variations to breed, with daytime highs of 92°F (33°C) and nighttime lows of 70°F (21°C). (Field temperatures taken in the habitat of this snake vary from 95°F [35°C] during the day to 62°F [17°C] at night.) The Institute of Herpetological Research (IHL) has found these temperature variations help decrease the number of respiratory problems that are typical of captive-kept white lips.

IHL has bred both the yellow and the black morphs. Babies of the black morphs are larger than the typical or "golden" form, and they feed more readily.

The sexes are placed together in January. No temperature fluctuations other than the 92/70 regimen are employed, and the 12/12 day/night schedule is unchanged. Females begin to show signs of being gravid in March or April, and the males are removed from the cages at that time. Eight to 15 eggs are laid from March to June. IHS removes the eggs for incubation despite the females' vigorous efforts to prevent this.

After about 60 days of incubation, the hatchlings emerge. Because they are so nervous and aggressive toward each other and their keeper, it is best to house each one separately. Some time (six to eight weeks) should elapse before the young are hungry; a few may wait three to four months before feeding on their own. Reluctant feeders may be tempted with a fuzzy mouse, skink, or gecko.

Care Notes: Neonates of the white-lipped python are especially susceptible to respiratory problems. This may be related to their original habitat; like blood pythons, they may have adapted to high humidities and are susceptible to respiratory infections when the humidity is too low. Be sure you keep the hatchlings warm enough; they need to be kept above 80°F (27°C) for at least their first 6 months.

The humidity-adapted white-lipped may have trouble shedding its entire skin. If patches of the old skin adhere, a two- to three-hour soak in warm to tepid water will loosen those portions so they can be removed. Captives offered a hide box filled with damp sphagnum will spend a great deal of time in the box. Dave and Tracy Barker of Vida Preciosa, Inc., have noted the improved skin conditions of the white lips offered this option.

Water Pythons
(*Liasis* spp.)

Liasis once contained several python species. But a recent reevaluation of the genus by taxonomist Arnold Kluge split *Liasis* and moved some examples into other genera. This sort of reorganization might (or might not) last. For the time being, *Liasis* is a fairly small genus.

All the *Liasis* are water-going snakes and in the wild are found near watering holes or slow-moving streams. In captivity, the snakes will spend at least part of their time in water if one at least dishpan-sized area is provided.

The *Liasis* stay on the small side for pythons, most reaching a length of 6 to 8 feet (1.8–2 m). One member, the olive python, *Liasis olivaceous*, does get larger, generally maxing out at 13 feet (3.9 m). The largest recorded length is 15 feet (4.6 m).

These are nervous pythons, needing a hide box or hiding area on a consistent basis. Their disposition ranges from fairly tolerable to consistently foul, a factor you may want to consider when dealing with a snake with a striking range of 3 feet (91 cm). Most herpetoculturists who work with the different species of *Liasis* point out that consistent, scheduled handling and tolerance of individual snakes' quirks will go a long way toward producing a tractable snake.

Liasis spp. feed on mice and other small to good-sized rodents. All seem to be aggressive feeders, feeding on turtles, birds, other snakes slightly smaller than they are, and mammals. Captives thrive on laboratory rodents and chicks. The downside of feeding chicks is that the snakes that consume chicks seem to have messier stools than those that feed on mammals.

Brown Water Python
(*Liasis fuscus*)

(This is a species of questionable validity. See also *Liasis mackloti*)

Not everyone loves the brown water python, primarily due to its irascible disposition. The young are eager and nervous biters but most adults mature into fairly docile snakes, if handled on a consistent basis. One reason why you may want to tame your brown water python is because of its behavior when disturbed. When nervous or excited, these snakes will defecate and thrash their tail at the same time, liberally coating everything around them.

Appearance: The brown water python is brown to brownish-black, paling to yellow-cream on the venter. The eyes are dark; the chin is white. The snout is broad and the head only slightly broader than the neck and body. The entire snake has a typical opalescent sheen.

Size: Females are slightly larger than the males, averaging 57 inches (147 cm) as compared to males at 51 inches (130 cm). A large brown water python is 8 feet (2.4 m). Hatchlings are 16 inches (42 cm).

Of moderate size, the brown water python (Liasis fuscus) *is considered only a color phase of Macklot's python by some taxonomists (see also photo on page 68).*

Range: The brown water python is found in a northcentral band across the northern edge of Australia; from Cornwallis Island in the Torres Strait; and eastern Irian Jaya, and western Papua.

Habitat: Near water, from streams, ponds, lakes, marshes, wet forests and flood plain drainages. Radiotelemetry studies have shown that the brown water python tends to stay in one area and forages for whatever food it can find in that spot at the time. It may eat rats during the dry season and waterfowl during the wet. Large females regularly prey on the eggs of water geese. One brown water python has been found in a tree, approaching a colony of bats, but as a rule, *fuscus* does not climb.

Breeding: Brown water pythons will breed in November through January when temperatures vary from 87 to 89°F (30–33°C) during the day and 60 to 65°F (16–18°C) at night. The females deposit their eggs from January through March and the neonates emerge from March to mid-June. Egg count ranges from eight to twelve, with the average being ten.

Some brown python females will thermoregulate their eggs by shivering;

other females will not. When artificially incubated, the incubation period is 59 to 63 days at 88 to 90°F (31–33°C).

Neonates will bite readily but the bites seem more driven by nerves than by hunger. The babies won't feed until they are about four to five months old. The Barkers have had all their hatchlings feed voluntarily at this age.

Care Notes: *Fuscus* eats mammals, birds, and reptiles, and the fact that it stays in one region in the wild suggests it is an opportunistic feeder, meaning it will eat almost anything it happens across. As with other water-going pythons, brown water pythons seem prone to respiratory infections. The young are irritable and should be maintained separately until regular feeding patterns have been established. Fuzzy or pinky mice are accepted as prey items by hatchlings. Hatchlings that seem reluctant to feed, especially after their first shed, may be tempted into trying a mouse if you scent the mouse with a skink or gecko.

Macklot's Python (*Liasis mackloti*)

Kluge has synonymized Macklot's python (*Liasis mackloti*) and the brown water python (*Liasis fuscus*). We have placed them in separate species accounts, because of their distinct geographical distributions and morphological differences. We personally feel that *Liasis* is a valid species.

Appearance: Macklot's python is dark brown-green above, paling to ocher laterally, and to white ventrally. The white coloration extends upward onto the lower and upper labials. Some Indonesian examples have an ocher-colored head and the dark dorsal coloration is liberally speckled with ocher scales; others from this same region may repeat the pattern, but employ a dark gray on pale gray coloration. The eyes are pale gray.

Macklot's python (Liasis m. mackloti) *is of moderate size and variable disposition. It has not yet become an American favorite.*

Size: To 6 feet (1.8 m).

Range: Southeast Indonesia.

Habitat: Forested areas, wet savannas, and river basins.

Breeding: Male Macklot's will engage in male-male sparring and constriction during the breeding season, even when there is no female present. The usual python breeding trigger of temperature variation will induce copulation during the breeding season of November through March. Breeding usually occurs at night. Once gravid, the females stop feeding until after egg deposition.

Eggs are laid from April into the first part of June. Clutch size is 8 to 14 eggs, and females allowed to maternally incubate will maintain incubation temperatures at 85 to 88°F (29–30°C) by thermoregulatory muscle contractions. When the cage temperature is 88°F (30°C) or higher, the female will loosen her coils and stop the contractions.

Incubation period is about 60 days, with the young emerging from June to September. When artificial incubation and a higher incubation temperature (89 to 91°F [31.7–33°C]) is used, hatching occurs a few days sooner, after 56 days of incubation, but this temperature is very close to the critical maximum temperature for other pythons.

Care Notes: These snakes adjust well to captivity and seem to prefer either rodents or fowl as food items. They do seem susceptible to respiratory and eye infections, especially if cage hygiene is less than perfect. The susceptibility may also be due to the fact that these are high-humidity pythons, and caging conditions that are too arid take their toll. The fine line between humid and too humid needs to be determined, and this information shared with other herpetoculturists.

The young are irritable and should be maintained separately until regular feeding patterns have been established. Fuzzy or pinky mice are accepted as prey items by hatchlings.

Sawu Python
(*Liasis mackloti savuensis*)

The Sawu python is from the small island of Sawu, in the Pacific. The confusion in the snake's common name (Sawu) as opposed to its scientific name (savuensis) is easily explained by languages. Latin, the language of taxonomy, has no "w," and the only way to write the island name (Sawu) is Savu.

Known only since 1993, the Sawu python was once thought to be a distinct species. Currently it is considered a race of the large and more aggressive Macklot's python, but taxonomists may alter this designation as further studies are made.

Appearance: The Sawu python has a base color of coral, overlaid with a dense speckling of gray scales. Hatchling Sawus are a brighter terra cotta with a white dorsum. As they mature, a darker gray suffusion darkens the dorsal scales. The quite startling eyes have pale to white irides.

Size: The largest examples are almost 5 feet long (152 cm). Most of the Sawus in the pet trade are either

Orange when a hatchling, the little Sawu python (Liasis mackloti savuensis) assumes a dark flecked, olive-gray coloration as an adult.

Although two subspecies of the big olive python are known, only the nominate form, Liasis o. olivaceus, *is prominent in herpetoculture.*

sexually mature adults at 3 feet (91 cm), or hatchlings at just over one foot in length (31 cm).

Range: The island of Sawu, west of Timor, Indonesia.

Habitat: Woodlands. This snake is found almost everywhere on the island, which is just 160 square miles (257 km).

Breeding: Each clutch contains fewer than a half-dozen fairly large eggs. Although the numbers of Sawus available are limited, the usual python breeding regimen of separation, cooling, reuniting the sexes, and misting/warming seems to work in triggering reproductive behavior. Eggs laid by wild-caught females were incubated successfully for 60 days at 88°F (30°C).

Care Notes: Sawu pythons in captivity so far have proven to adapt well to life in a terrarium with a hiding area, water dish, hot spot, and climbing limb. Because these snakes are found in such a limited area in the wild, it is important that breeding programs be set up to make the captive populations self-maintaining. Unlike other members of the genus, the Sawu python is not ready to bite, eager to expel the contents of its musk glands, or to thrash around when held. This quiet, rather small-sized snake with its baleful white

eyes seems to have the potential to make a very nice pet snake—the only disadvantages are the high price and very limited availability!

Olive Python
(*Liasis olivaceous*)

The olive python is infrequently seen in the pet market; few are available either from wholesalers or from breeders. The very limited supply available is partially due to the limited demand—many hobbyists don't want to deal with a fair-sized snake that bites at essentially every opportunity (the tractable examples may *occasionally* pass up the chance to bite)—and to the trade restrictions on Australian wildlife.

Appearance: Olive green to olive brown dorsally, lighter ventrally. The pale-to-white coloration includes both upper and lower labials. Heat sensory pits are along the lower labials.

Size: 8 to 13 inches (243–396 cm), rarely 15 feet (4.57 m). Hatchlings are about 24 inches (61 cm) at birth.

Range: Australia

Habitat: In the wild, the olive python is found in rocky escarpments and river gorges of the northern and western coastal districts.

Breeding: Four breeding records for the olive python in Australia report matings from mid-May to mid-September (their fall season), followed by egg depositions in September and October (spring in Australia). Incubation periods ranged from 85 to 95 days, spread from late November to late January. Clutch size may be up to 40 eggs, but averages about 16.

Breeding records in America, for an 8-foot (2.4 m) male and a 10-foot (3 m) female, record oviposition in March. After 79 to 81 days of incubation, hatchlings emerged in June. The young fed aggressively, and birds were sometimes preferred as the first food items.

Cannibalism has not been reported from this species, but husbandry records are scarce and breeding records even more so. Given the records for the genus, maintaining separate quarters seems prudent, especially for the young.

Care Notes: Native food items for the olive python include wallabies, bushrat bandicoots, birds, and occasionally lizards, another good reason (aside from legalities) to purchase only captive-born stock.

New World Python
(*Loxocemus bicolor*)

This python "misfit" is the only python found in the New World. Taxonomists cannot agree exactly how this python is related to other snakes, much less its exact degree of "pythonicity." It has been classified a xenopeltid, a relative of the Asian sunbeam snake. It has also been placed with the aniilids, a poorly known group of burrowing snakes found further south in Latin America. A third approach simply creates a brand new family, Loxocemidae, for this single species, while yet another approach snatches this snake back from the python grouping and places it within the boas in a subfamily Loxoceminae.

Appearance: This snake superficially resembles a rather elongated sand boa or rubber boa, with dark brown scales on the dorsal side and white scales on the venter. The scales have a faint opalescent sheen. The nose bears an enlarged rostral scale.

Size: Adults may reach 4 feet (1.22 m) in length; most are a bit smaller, to 3 to 3½ feet (90–107 cm).

Origin: Mexico.

Range/Habitat: This snake is a burrowing snake that pokes through soft soil in search of food items. It feeds on mammals that it immobilizes by pressing against the walls of its burrow. It may leave its burrow very late at night. In the states of Colima and Chiapas we have found this snake crossing sandy roadways after midnight.

Breeding: This secretive python is not well known in captivity. A few wild-caught females in our collection have laid small clutches of large eggs, but the eggs have so far failed to hatch. Others have had more success with this quiet snake.

Care Notes: A tank with several inches of peat topsoil or cypress mulch will permit these secretive snakes to burrow. Add an untippable water container and occasionally mist the substrate. Offer prekilled mice or small rats.

Morelia: Carpet Pythons and Relatives

Scrub Python
(*Morelia amethystina*)

The scrub python is a big, moderately attractive snake with a very unattractive disposition. It is one of the few snakes with chromogenic abilities, paling distinctly from day to nighttime. Although it is a member of *Morelia* at present, it has also been placed in the past in *Liasis* and *Python*. It is a favored aboriginal food item in its Australian homeland and in Papua New Guinea.

Appearance: The body scales of the scrub python impart a coarse,

Not even taxonomists can agree on whether the snake we refer to as the New World python (Loxocemus bicolor) *is truly a python.*

Although some populations of the scrub python (Morelia amethystina) *remain of moderate size, it is generally conceded that this species of pythons is one of the four largest.*

26 eggs in December (mid-summer). Incubation at 84 to 88°F (28–31°C) was 105 to 108 days.

American breeding records reveal copulation in October with deposition in December, and copulation in May with oviposition in July. Incubation at 88 to 90°F (31–33°C) yielded hatchlings in 83 and 87 days. Females allowed maternal incubation will demonstrate thermogenesis by shivering; one female incubating her eggs would leave them each day to bask in a warm spot, and not return to coil around her eggs until the next day.

There is no data on whether temperature cycling was used to induce breeding. Australian records also indicate extremely aggressive male-male sparring during breeding season.

The young are quiet snakes, but this behavior largely disappears after the first shed, one to two weeks after hatching. The neonates generally feed three to ten weeks after shedding. Mammals, birds, and lizards are consumed.

Care Notes: As its name indicates, the scrub python occurs under dry conditions, which is the way its caging should be maintained. The cage needs to be big, with a hide box big enough for the entire snake, elevated perches, and a large water bowl. Captives eat rodents, birds, and rabbits. Use caution when you feed these snakes, especially the larger specimens; they can easily strike a third of their length. Dave and Tracy Barker of VPI (Vida Preciosa, Inc.) feel that these snakes can learn maintenance routines and will associate particular keeper actions with food, so conversely they will learn *not* to aggressively lunge toward the door the moment the cage is opened.

Boelen's Python (*Morelia boeleni*)

This snake is one of the most protected animals in Papua New Guinea.

rough look to the snake, and the interstices between the scales are dark and prominent. The large head is covered with big, flat, platelike scales, and the head is distinct from the neck. Color combinations vary from dark olive and dark-brown to orange and ocher to brown with silver and any combination thereof. The dorsum may be crossed with darker saddles, bars, or vague splotches. Green iridescence appears between the coils in folds of skin. Older, larger specimens are heavy-bodied snakes.

Size: Adults can reach 15 feet (4.6 m); the record length is slightly more than 27 feet (8.2 m). Hatchlings are 23 inches (58 cm) at birth .

Origin: The scrub python is from northeastern Queensland, Australia; Papua New Guinea; and Indonesia.

Range/Habitat: This snake is found near beach fronts, in dry sclerophyll forest (scrublands) and rain forests.

Breeding: The large size of this snake and its unpleasant disposition means there is little demand for even captive-bred specimens. Breeding records from Australia indicate breeding in September through October (their spring), and oviposition of 8 to

Only recently has it become available, and the few Boelen's that do appear on lists command prices in the several thousand-dollar range. Although various zoos and private breeding institutions are working with this snake, reproductive strategies have not yet been determined. As time goes on and more is known about breeding these beautiful enigmatic snakes, their availability will increase.

Appearance: This is a stocky python with a big, wide head that is distinct from the narrow neck. The snake is a shimmering blue-black on the dorsum, and pale lemon yellow ventrally. The labials are vertically barred with black and yellow, giving a toothy smile look to the snake at first glance. To add to the contrast, a series of narrow yellow bars juts upwards on each side from the belly, but do not connect over the back. The underbelly darkens posteriorly to black.

Size: Heavy-bodied, 6 to 8 feet (1.83–2.4 m). A maximum size has not been reported, but individuals who encounter this snake in the wild may confuse its girth and general heaviness and report a snake much larger than reality.

Origin: New Guinea.

Habitat: Rain forest above 3,280 feet (1,000 m), in humid, low light conditions. At these elevations Boelen's are a cool temperature python.

Breeding: Some of the first Boelen's pythons in the United States were maintained at the Dallas Zoo, but without breeding success. Now at least eight U.S. zoos have active breeding programs for these snakes, including the Cincinnati Zoo (with two pairs), Oklahoma City Zoo (two males, one female) and the Dallas and Fort Worth zoos (a pair each).

Small numbers of Boelen's pythons are in private breeding collections such as VPI (Dave and Tracy Barker). Although a few gravid females have

Boelen's python (Morelia boeleni) *is a seldom-seen and difficult-to-breed species from the remote New Guinean highlands.*

been imported, no actual reproduction of the animals in private breeders' collections has been reported. The eggs from gravid imported females have been incubated with varying degrees of success; the young are quite different in appearance from the adults, being reddish with white markings. Clutch size, as reported from nests in Papua New Guinea, averages 14 eggs.

Care Notes: Captive Boelen's feed on laboratory rodents and small rabbits. Examples from the wild are thought to include ground-nesting birds in their diet.

These high-humidity snakes may have trouble shedding in lower humidity conditions; misting the snake or increasing the humidity of the cage just before shedding may aid in the process. Although usually encountered in terrestrial conditions, Boelen's that have been spotted in the wild climb readily.

The babies are more skittish than the adults, striking at anything that could possibly be either predator or prey. Adults, once accustomed to a cage routine that offers food on one set routine and cage cleaning on another routine, settle down and become fairly calm snakes. Do not take this friendship for granted; simply look at the heavy jaws and the weight of the snake to remind yourself!

Centralian Python
(*Morelia bredli*)

Although some taxonomists may consider *bredli* a subspecies of *M. spilota*, many herpetologists do not. The problem is, of course, in agreeing on what forms a species and what forms a subspecies, and it doesn't seem as though there will ever be agreement on that issue.

The Centralian python is a geographically distinct population, with consistent morphological differences from the carpet pythons. The most obvious is in scalation, both in size and count. *M. bredli* has smaller scales, both in dorsal body scale count and in head scale counts.

Appearance: These reddish snakes have ocher-colored intermittent bars across their bodies, in general conformation looking like a diamond or carpet but with a brighter, richer coloring. They are reddish in overall coloration, with the paler bars forming incomplete or solid lines over the back. The coloration darkens posteriorly. Heat sensory pits are on the front upper labials and the lower posterior labials. The labials are white. The tongue is dark blue.

Size: Adult at 5 feet to 6½ feet (1.5–1.98 m)

Range: The Centralian python comes from a small horseshoe-shaped region in the southern sector of the Northern Territory, Australia.

Habitat: *Bredli* is a secretive snake and has been found in trees and shrubs in river drainages, in dry river beds; in rocky outcrops and in deep crevices; in caves.

Breeding: The Centralian python seems to be a spring-breeding python, probably due to the very cold wintertime temperatures in its range. Eggs are deposited in the early summer, and hatch in mid- to late summer. Eggs that were incubated at 85 to 87°F (29–31°C) hatched in 67 days. Average clutch size is 23 eggs. The neonates were not interested in pinkies, and it is postulated that lizards such as geckos and skinks may make up a major portion of the younger snakes' diets.

Like other pythons, the young are nervous captives, ready to bite and quick to react to an encroaching hand. Adults, on the other hand, are more placid, adjusting to captivity and handling with equanimity.

As far as we know, this snake is kept in only a few breeding programs in Australia.

Care Notes: These snakes are mammal- and bird-feeders, and in captivity will usually switch over to mice and birds with no problems. There seems to be some reluctance to consume rats; try gerbils or hamsters as alternate food sources.

Rough-scaled Python
(*Morelia carinata*)

Since this snake is known from fewer than a half-dozen specimens, none of which are in captivity, most of our information about its habits is extrapolated from what we know about other *Morelia* species from western Australia.

Appearance: Although this snake superficially resembles the lookalikes Centralian and carpet pythons, a closer examination will reveal a combination of significant differences. Rough-scaled pythons have big heads, distinct from the neck; keeled scales; heat-sensory pits on the upper and lower labials; very small loreal scales (the scales between the eyes and the snout); and a large frontal scale (the central scale between the eyes).

The overall pattern consists of dark blotches against a light base color; the blotches create an almost chainlike arrangement of the pale coloration. No black coloration is visible on any of the four specimens that have been collected or photographed, which serves as another distinguishing characteristic to set this snake apart from the Centralian or carpet pythons.

Size: About 6 feet (1.8 m).

Origin: All four specimens were found in a single river drainage near the northern coast of western Australia.

Range/Habitat: These snakes are found in forested areas in boulder-strewn gorges. Two specimens that were photographed in the wild were found in trees; the other two specimens are from the preserved collection at the Western Australian Museum. These last two examples were collected in 1976 and 1987.

The habitat of the rough-scaled python is a relic monsoon forest, scattered portions of which still exist in Australia, but the existence of which is threatened by increasingly dry conditions. Wild population levels of this snake are completely unknown.

Breeding: This snake is unknown in captivity, but the usual breeding regime for pythons would probably be applicable.

Care Notes: The adult snake photographed by researcher John Wiegel was in a fruiting tree, posed about a yard above the ground in head-down ambush position. This is typical of pythons that feed on nocturnal mammals, so we can guess that the rough-scaled python feeds on small ground-running rodents and other warm-blooded prey.

Oenpelli Python
(*Morelia oenpelliensis*)

The Oenpelli python, although evidently not rare within its home range, was not described as a distinct species until 1977. These little-known pythons can change color; and this is most pronounced at night when the snakes change from tan with brown blotches to pale taupe or silver gray. This is the largest of the *Morelia* clan, and is a rock-dweller. Most examples have been found on the ground.

Appearance: Pale reddish-tan with longitudinal blotches, arranged in four to six disjunct stripes. The blotches are darker brown, and the pattern becomes less distinct posteriorly. The belly is pale cream, shading to taupe at the sides. The long head has somewhat protruding eyes that obtain forward vision along a slight concavity that runs from the eye to the snout. Hatchlings are very slender, long snakes.

Size: About 9 to 13 feet (3–4 m), with a reported 15.5 feet (4.6 m) maximum. The two live hatchlings were 32 and 35 inches (83 and 90 cm) and shed 66 and 75 days after hatching. Both fed on live finches five days after shedding.

Range: Northern tip of the Northern Territory, Australia.

Habitat: Sandstone and rocky outcrops near river drainages, evidently either on the ground or in trees. Although this snake is largely terrestrial due to its size and weight, some Oenpelli have been found in trees laden with overripe fruit, evidently waiting for the pigeons and fruit bats that visit these trees. Oenpelli have also been found sheltering in deep rock cracks, hollow trees, and in caves.

Breeding: Very few of these snakes are in captivity. Gravid females, both wild-caught and long-term examples, may lay fertile eggs, but the eggs fail to hatch. A variety of reasons have been offered for the failure to hatch, but no single explanation seems to fit. Another member of *Morelia*, the green tree python, has long been known for the low hatching rate of fertile eggs.

Hatchlings of all of the races of the carpet python are less colorful than the adults. This intergrade M. s. cheynei x M. s. spilota *will be a beautiful olive-black and yellow when adult.*

Current work with the green tree suggests that a temperature drop during the final week of incubation may serve as a hatching signal for the embryos; perhaps temperature changes during incubation would increase the hatching rate of the Oenpelli python.

Care Notes: Captive Oenpelli pythons feed on birds (doves, pigeons, chickens, and guinea hens) and mice, rats, and rabbits. Most seem to readily feed on birds, and only reluctantly feed on rodents. Tying a bird onto a rodent may increase its acceptability.

The Oenpelli python is evidently a calm snake, with even wild adults rarely biting during capture. The establishment of captive breeding populations is an eagerly awaited phenomenon. This will take a number of years, due to the few specimens in captivity and the protective attitude of Australia toward its native wildlife.

Carpet Pythons
(*Morelia spilota* ssp.)

The carpet pythons are Australian and New Guinean pythons that are divided into six subspecies. Where ranges overlap, intergradations between the subspecies are known to

occur. Efforts to describe populations within the group began as early as 1984, but so far suggestions to elevate the taxa to full specific levels have not been successful. Only two of these, the coastal and jungle carpets, are seen with any frequency in the United States. A third subspecies, the diamond python, is one of the most coveted of all snakes in American herpetoculture. Only these three subspecies will be discussed here. Breeding techniques and behavior patterns of all the subspecies are essentially the same.

Diamond Python
(*Morelia s. spilota*)

The diamond python is a small (about 6 feet [1.8 m]) and slender species from eastern New South Wales. Unlike its carpet python relatives, some of which have been bred in captivity with relative ease, this was not true of the diamond python.

Appearance: Diamonds are black snakes with yellow tipping on dorsal and lateral scales. Yellow diamonds are enclosed in patches of jet black on the sides. The subspecies is cream to yellow ventrally. Hatchlings are brown with indeterminate buff markings, looking so much like any of the other baby carpet pythons that the close alliances are unmistakable.

Size: Adults range from 6 to 7½ feet (1.8–2.3 m).

Range: Australia, from the eastern part of New South Wales.

Habitat: Forest edges, forest clearing, river edges, and rocky ledges, where they feed on small rodents and marsupials. During the winter, diamond pythons are commonly found near or in human dwellings in New South Wales. They may be underneath or in the rafters of poultry sheds, or in the attics or in the crawl spaces of homes.

Breeding: Within their range, there is a notable variation in seasonal temperature. Some summer days reach into the 90s°F (33–35°C), and winter temperatures can drop to freezing (0°C). Both sexes are inactive during cold weather, seeking shelter on the coldest days and on most nights. The winter shelter can be in human dwellings, but more frequently is on sunny, north-oriented escarpments.

In the spring the snakes become active and the males begin prowling, looking for sexually receptive females. The males may wander considerable distances in this process. Once they encounter a female, mating occurs and the males begin wandering again. Unlike carpet pythons, males do not engage in combat.

The gravid females seek nesting areas, often in grassy woodland openings along streams. They use their neck, curved in a J-shape, to scrape together a nest of leaves, and deposit their eggs in the debris. Females remain with the eggs, incubating them in their coils, only leaving to warm up in a patch of sun before returning and re-coiling around the eggs.

One of the first American hobbyists to successfully breed diamond pythons was Stan Chiras. He succeeded only after cooling his diamond pythons almost to the point of hibernation. Since his success, other hobbyists have followed his example, and today diamond pythons are almost routinely bred by advanced herpetoculturists.

Diamonds lay clutches of up to 50 eggs, although 16 to 25 is more normal. Incubation of 88 to 92°F (31–34°C) seems to be the norm, with eggs hatching in about 60 days.

Care Notes: Diamond pythons like areas of seclusion, both on the floor of the cage and in an elevated hide box. They will eat a variety of small rodents. Adults are fairly docile; the young are nippy until they settle down to a routine and become more adept at identifying food and enemies. The

The diamond python, Morelia s. spilota, *is the most coveted, expensive, and difficult to breed of the several races of the Australian carpet pythons.*

young may not recognize pinkies as food; try jumpers (furred young mice with the eyes barely open) instead.

Jungle Carpet Python (*Morelia s. cheynei*)

The jungle carpet python has the smallest range of the species. They are fairly small, slender-bodied, with large heads.

Background coloration is pale, with black-edged dark blotches alternating with the paler yellow-to-cream base color. Dorsal areas of both elements tend to darken with age. The overall effect is a banded pattern. The eyes are dark and the tongue is blue.

The jungle carpets don't seem to get more than 5½ feet (1.67 m) long, although some examples from the Atherton rain forest may reach more than 8 feet (2.4 m). Captive-maintained specimens may reach a greater size than wild examples, but the lineage of most captive carpet pythons is too muddled to identify the exact subspecies.

Rivers and waterways that drain Australia's Atherton tableland form the heart of the range of the jungle carpet

The small, brightly colored, "jungle" variety of the carpet python is now known subspecifically as Morelia spilota cheynei.

The breeding regime is much like that for other carpets, including wintertime cooling and reduction of photoperiod. Reintroduction of the sexes is followed by copulation, basking, and ovulation. Egg deposition is about 40 days after ovulation, and hatching occurs about 54 days after deposition. The young are 16 inches (42 cm) at hatching. Some breeders separate the sexes, but we have not found it necessary in Florida.

Coastal Carpet Python (*Morelia s. mcdowelli*)

This is the largest and most varied of the carpet pythons, and is one of the most commonly available in the United States.

The coastal carpet is dark dorsally, paler ventrally, with 60 to 80 dark-edged pale blotches arranged evenly from head to tail. The labials are pale to white, but the head pattern is indistinct.

The coastal carpet ranges from 6 to 8 feet (1.8–2.4 m). On rare occasions, some may reach 14 feet (4.3 m), but there's a strong natural selection against snakes living long enough to grow that large.

The snake is found from the Cape York Peninsula to Coffs Harbor, NSW. It is most commonly encountered in heavily timbered areas or in the upper rafters of chicken coops.

Breeding techniques include wintertime cooling and photoperiod reduction, separation and reintroduction of the sexes, and feeding only when the sexes are separated prior to repeated introduction. When the female is observed to ovulate or begin to bask with the lower half of her body turned upwards, the male is removed. Egg deposition of about 27 eggs occurs 44 days after ovulation or 25 days after the final shed. Incubation takes about 54 days, and can be as warm as 87 to 89°F (31–32°C).

python. Although their range includes some elevations of 5,300 feet (1,622 m), these snakes are found along river drainages that lead to the coast. They like dense subtropical rain forests, but much of the rain forest in the tableland area has been reduced to disjunct corridors. Within their preferred habitat, the jungle pythons are arboreal. In captivity, they mate and feed from elevated perches.

The coastal carpet python (Morelia spilota mcdowelli) *is the largest and least colorful of the commonly seen races. This is an unusual striped variant.*

Green Tree Python
(*Morelia viridis*)

Known for years as *Chondropython viridis,* the scientific name was changed in 1994 to *Morelia viridis,* to reflect its close relationship with carpet pythons. However, many hobbyists and professionals alike have continued to use the common name "chondro python." Some hobbyists might consider this snake one of the "choice" pythons, due to its attractive appearance and manageable adult size, but its cost, snappy temperament, and specialized regimen of care make it a snake for the experienced keeper who doesn't mind being bitten on a consistent basis.

Appearance: The most typical adult phase is a bright green, although blue or yellow examples are occasionally found. A series of white or blue dorsal and/or lateral spots is evident on most. Sometimes these light areas form an intermittent line down the dorsal surface. Examples from Aru Island are a deeper green coloration with powder blue lips and venter.

Hatchlings are extremely variable and in coloration may be light-years away from the adults. Hatching as brick red, lemon yellow, or brown babies (often all colors are found within the same clutch), with the characteristic intermittent white markings along the back, most change to the bright green of the adult. The color transformation may be rapid, beginning when the babies are only a few weeks old, or it may be slower. The changeover is completed by the time the young are two years old. A few remain solid lemon yellow their entire lives.

All have thermosensory pits along the upper and lower labials.

Size: While an unusually large specimen may measure 7 feet (2.1 m) in length, the green tree python generally reaches a 6-foot (1.8 m) length. This is a fairly slender snake, so a specimen coiled cinnamon bun-style across a branch may appear smaller than it actually is.

Range: In Papua and Irian Jaya, New Guinea and on the Cape York Peninsula of Australia.

Habitat: These arboreal snakes are found in elevations from sea level to 6,000 feet (1,850 m), which encompasses a wide range of habitat niches. Although these agile snakes are certainly arboreal, there's an increasing

Usually a bright green when adult, hatchlings of the green tree python Morelia (Chondropython) viridis, *may be russet, chocolate, or yellow (as seen here).*

body of evidence that they ground forage at night. During the day, sleeping green tree pythons can be found in sheltered tree hollows, secreted inside bromeliads, or on low branches. Unfortunately, wild-caught individuals arrive at the dealers without specific collection data, so replication of the original habit is at best guesswork.

Breeding: Generally, green tree pythons breed from late August to late December. Do not place two males together with the female; they will engage in male-male combat with serious damage to each other and anything else in the way at the time (including your hands and your face). This might be a propitious time to point out that green tree pythons have long front teeth that are useful for grabbing small furry or feathered animals. Their bite is painful and impressive, not only from the discomfort involved in gently peeling back the snake's jaws so you won't pull out any of its teeth, but also in the quantity of blood shed.

Eight to 12 eggs are laid from late November through February, sometimes in late April. Females need an elevated egg deposition box. Those not given elevated boxes will sometimes drop their eggs while draped across a tree limb.

Incubation, either maternal or artificial, is variable, from 39 to 65 days. If the female is permitted maternal incubation, she will coil around the eggs. In northern areas, she will begin thermoregulatory contractions if the cage temperature falls below 84°F (28°C).

In southern areas like Florida, acclimatized green tree pythons will breed whenever the temperature is cool enough. If the room temperature is cool (82 to 85°F [28–29°C]), maternal incubation can be allowed to take place. Monitor the actions of the female to ensure the eggs don't dry out. If you prefer to place the eggs in an incubator, be certain that ventilation is adequate, particularly during the last few weeks of incubation. Some breeders now feel that increased ventilation and a slight drop in incubation temperature during the last week of incubation provides the "time to pip out" stimulus that otherwise results in full-term eggs that inexplicably fail to hatch.

Care Notes: This is an arboreal snake that seems to prefer to perch on branches, rather than PVC piping, to hang from. It needs warm temperatures and high humidity to feed.

Young green tree pythons seem very susceptible to irreversible tail kinking. The problem is evidently due to delicate vertebrae in the tail, which can be dislocated by simple actions such as immobilizing the tail tip when using a probe to determine the snake's sex, offering too heavy a prey item, resulting in too great a tension on the tail as the item is taken and eaten, or manually everting the hemipenes on a hatchling.

Newborns can be difficult feeders, but generally can be started on pinky mice. If they resist the pinkies, try starting them on lizards or frogs. Attaching a few chicken feathers to the pink mouse might be helpful. Adults will feed on birds (chicks) or on rodents.

The green tree python and the South American emerald tree boa (*Corallus caninus*) look very much like one another to the inexperienced eye, and they occupy the same ecological niche in their respective countries. There are some distinguishing factors. Tree boas have bigger heads; the snout is elongated and the head has a flatter appearance. In contrast, the green tree python has a sculpted, more compact head. The emerald tree boa has ladderlike vertebral markings, as opposed to the broken-line vertebral stripe of the green tree python.

Angolan Python
(*Python anchietae*)

These little-known snakes have different scalation than most other pythons. The scales on the head, instead of being large and platelike, are small and granular, feeling more like rounded beads to the touch than slick, flattened scales.

The Angolan pythons enjoy a magnitude of protection little experienced by other python species. In the northern part of their range, in Angola, there has been a civil war for over 20 years, and members of the rebel forces have liberally scattered land mines in untold numbers and locations. To the south, in Namibia, the snakes are legally protected from snake hunters, and the snakes themselves are something of a country symbol. Legal exportation is extremely difficult.

Appearance: Adults are dark chocolate brown with intermittent dark-edged light bars and vertebral spots. A light stripe runs from the nosetip along the temporals. Hatchlings are dark chocolate with lemon yellow markings.

Size: Adults are small, measuring just 50 to 60 inches (127–154 cm). Hatchlings are about 17 inches (43 cm) long after their first shed.

Origin: Africa, the countries of Angola and Namibia

Range/Habitat: Rocky escarpments characterized by little annual rain (4 to 10 inches [10–25 cm]) and very hot days. Some nights are below freezing in the wintertime. These snakes are certainly capable of hiding in rocky areas and are probably selectively nocturnal when the weather warrants it.

Breeding: The Barkers' Angolan pythons bred at three years of age. Typical python December-to-May copulations were triggered by reduced photoperiod and temperatures. In May the female ovulated, with the typical mid-body swelling that lasted less than 48 hours. After ovulation the pair was not placed together again. The female shed a week after ovulation and began to bask under her hot spot extensively, often with the posterior two-thirds of her body upside down. Six very large eggs were deposited in the egg box in early July, 28 days after the female's last ecdysis. The female coiled about her eggs and began maternal incubation with thermoregulatory shivering. Cage temperature was 83°F (28°C); after a few minutes of shivering, the temperature inside her coils rose to 88°F (31°C).

The decision was made to remove and incubate the eggs. When weighed, the combined weight of the eggs was 49 percent of the female, indicating the energy and effort required to produce the eggs. The female fed two days after laying the eggs.

The eggs were incubated at 90°F (32.2°C). After 58 days, all six hatched, two males and four females. Although the young were ready feeders, they were not aggressive snakes and did not object to being handled. All fed readily on fuzzy mice.

Care Notes: These appear to be calm, easygoing pythons that feed

The seldom seen Angolan python (Python anchietae) *is as rare in herpetoculture as its relative the ball python is common.*

Although fairly new in herpetoculture, the rather quietly colored Borneo short-tailed python (Python curtus breitensteini) has become a hobby favorite.

readily on fuzzies and adult mice or rats. The Barkers estimate that perhaps 20 pairs are in captivity, and it may be a while before most of us have the opportunity to keep these engaging snakes ourselves.

Short-Tailed Pythons
(*Python curtus* ssp.)

Until the 1990s only one subspecies of the short-tailed python (*Python curtus* ssp.) was imported into the United States. This was the blood python (*P. curtus brongersmai*), from the northern and central areas of Sumatra.

A second subspecies, the Sumatran short-tailed python (*P. c. curtus*), is found in southern and western Sumatra. The third subspecies, the Borneo short-tailed python (*P. c. breitsteini*) is found on the island of Borneo, to the east of Sumatra.

These snakes are geographically isolated from each other (the Sumatran subspecies are separated by a mountain chain) but their care regimen is the same. Using the blood python as our primary example, let's look at the short-tailed python group.

Blood Python
(*Python curtus brongersmai*)

Most of the beautifully patterned and colored blood pythons exported from Sumatra leave that country as skins, not as pets. Each year some 60,000 of the darker morphs are turned into shoes, boots, belts, purses, and clothing. Several hundred of the brighter red morphs, the ones for whom the common name "blood" was coined, are exported annually for the pet trade.

Appearance: At first glance the blood python looks like an outrageously obese snake. At second glance you notice the beautifully mottled blotches of red, orange, yellow, and tan, and the paler blotches on the sides that are peppered with minute black dots. The head is flat and large. The tongue is usually black. The eyes are small, and in the blood python, no small rows of scales (called suboculars) separate the eye from the upper labials. In both the other subspecies, the Borneo and Sumatran short-tailed pythons, the lower edge of the eye is separated from the upper labials by a ring of smaller scales, the suboculars. Only the blood python has the characteristic red coloration; both the other subspecies are mottled in shades of brown, tan, gray, and black.

Size: Blood pythons are sexually mature at 3½ to 4 feet (1.1–1.2 m). Larger snakes may reach 10 feet (3.1 m). Hatchlings are 12 to 16 inches (30–41 cm).

The Borneo short-tailed python and the Sumatran short-tailed python are smaller, never exceeding 5 feet (1.5 m). Their hatchlings are just slightly smaller than the blood python, at 10 to 13 inches (25–32 cm).

Range: The blood python is found over much of Southeast Asia. It is found in Bangkok, Banga Island, and the islands of Singapore, Pinang, and north and central Sumatra.

The Borneo short-tailed python is found on the island of Borneo; the Sumatran short-tailed python is found in southern and western Sumatra.

Habitat: These snakes spend at least part of their time in marshy areas with high humidity, and, of all the pythons, seem to need these conditions duplicated for successful husbandry. Blood pythons are extremely susceptible to repeated respiratory infections if their caging is too small or not humid enough.

Breeding: Although young and hatchling Borneo and Sumatran short-tailed pythons are available, not much work has been done specifically on their captive propagation. Until then, it seems likely that the guidelines used in breeding the blood python could be successfully extrapolated to its conspecifics.

In North America, blood pythons mate from January to April. Although temperature fluctuations play a role in triggering this behavior, this snake seems to require less of a fluctuation than some other python species. Instead, the key is day length.

During the summer, day lengths need to be about 15 hours. Begin decreasing the amount of day light to 9 hours per day (see page 41 for this technique).

As the days are shorten, begin cooling. Most breeders use a cool daytime temperature of 83 to 85°F (28–29°C), and a nighttime temperature in the high 70s°F (24-25°C). A hot spot may or may not be utilized, but it seems prudent to offer the pythons a choice in thermoregulation.

Some breeders either drastically reduce the number and size of feedings from early December until March, or stop feeding the animals altogether during this time.

Snakes should be placed together in late December or January. They can be left with each other, or simply removed and reintroduced periodically. Copulation may occur numerous times; keep track of the dates, so you'll know when to expect eggs.

With the cooling period's end in February, the snakes' cage can be warmed to 86 to 88°F (29–32°C) in the day and 78 to 82°F (26–28°C) at night.

Successful copulation is indicated by ovulation, which occurs in March to April. The mid-body bulge is apparent for 24 hours.

Eggs are laid about 60 days after mating. Although the female Borneo short-tailed python (*P. c. breitensteini*) will incubate her eggs with thermoregulatory shivering, this has not yet been observed with the blood python or with the Sumatran short-tailed python.

Typical incubator conditions of 87 to 90°F (30–33°C) and 90 to 100 percent humidity seem adequate. The eggs hatch in 58 to 65 days.

Neonates shed much later than most python young, at 8 to 12 weeks. Although the young may feed before that first ecdysis, some breeders feel it unnecessary to offer food until the young are four weeks old and show an active interest in eating.

Heavy bodied and sometimes delicate, Python curtus brongersmai *is the most brightly colored subspecies of the blood (or short-tailed) python.*

Although usually somewhat smaller, the Burmese python (Python molurus bivitattus) *occasionally attains 20 feet (6 meters) in total length, and is* definitely *not a snake for all hobbyists.*

active (and feeding) during the night. Despite the fact that they are found near slow-moving streams or actually semisubmerged in the water, no fish component to their diet has been discovered. Captives feed on rodents, small mammals, and birds.

Burmese Pythons

Burmese Python
(*Python molurus bivittatus*)

The Burmese python group is actually three big snakes—the Burmese, the Indian, and the Ceylon pythons. All are subspecies of *Python bivitattus*, but each has its own common name and its own coterie of hobbyists. Of the three, the Burmese is the best known and most popular.

The gentle and docile nature of the Burmese—in addition to its beauty—is the main reason for its popularity as a pet snake or a breeder snake. Nonetheless, the snake gets BIG, and a big snake is more than the average hobbyist can handle. Unfortunately, the zoos and nature centers that might be remotely interested in a snake this large probably already have their specimens, gifts of other, earlier, hobbyists. Before you acquire a Burmese, it is important to give some thought to what you will do once it reaches 10 to 15 feet (3–4.6 m) in length.

Appearance: The normal coloration of the Burmese python is tan with dark-edged olive-brown dorsal and lateral blotches. A dark spearhead is present on the top of the head. This used to be the standard (and only) color pattern of the Burmese, but that has changed radically. With the acquisition of a few wild-caught albinos (which sold for five figures fifteen years ago), breeding programs have produced lineages of albinos, axanthic (lacking yellow pigment), a busy, convoluted pattern called labyrinth pattern, "green" coloration, and striped forms.

Care Notes: The important thing to remember when providing caging for a blood python, or indeed any short-tailed python, is to be guided by the animal's weight, not its comparatively small size. The cage needs to be as big as it would be for a thinner-bodied python of an equal weight. Make sure that the cage is long enough for your short-tailed python to stretch out almost its full length, and broad enough so it can turn around. Being able to stretch out seems to help avoid the respiratory infections that are chronic problems with blood pythons.

Another respiratory problem preventative seems to be humidity. Blood pythons do best in high-humidity cages, but good ventilation is a must. Reluctant feeders (usually adults from the wild) can sometimes be cajoled into feeding by duplicating the marshy environment where they ambush-feed in the wild. This can be done by providing a damp humus substrate (enough to burrow in), a large soaking bowl, and a hide box.

These are primarily nocturnal snakes, quiescent during the day and

Size: Adult at 7 to 10 feet (2.1–3 m), commonly attains 14 feet (4.3 m), and has been recorded at over 25 feet (7.6 m) long. Hatchlings are about 16 inches (41 cm). This is a heavy-bodied snake; the females tend to grow to a much larger size than the males.

Range: Burma, Malaysia, and Indonesia.

Habitat: The Burmese python is found in open fields, cultivated areas, and wooded areas. It is an adept swimmer.

Breeding: Successful breeding of the Burmese pythons may be as easy as placing the males and females together after cycling them. If no response is shown, gently mist the snakes in the evening. If this still doesn't evoke copulation, you may need to bring a second male into the enclosure to evoke territoriality. If you do this, be extremely careful. Sexually mature Burmese python males are very antagonistic toward each other, and wrestling bouts, feints, and bites are typical actions. Be prepared to remove the subordinate male should it become necessary; two people would make this process a lot safer.

The female, if pregnant, will put on considerable girth. Increase her feedings. Make sure that an egg deposition box, big enough for the female, the substrate, and the eggs, is inside the enclosure. The Burmese, in keeping with its size, lays large clutches of large eggs. Up to 60 eggs are laid each time.

Females will readily incubate their eggs, if allowed, and will coil around the eggs and raise the clutch's temperature by shivering. Artificial incubation is, for most breeders, less worrisome than watching over and trying to second-guess the female. Use the standardized temperatures and incubation length suggested on page 55.

Care Notes: This docile snake feeds well on mice, rats, rabbits, and chick-

Hobbyists have developed strains of the Burmese python (Python molurus bivittatus) in numerous odd colors and patterns. This is a striped phase of normal coloration.

ens or other birds. Many keepers don't intend to maintain a snake as large as a Burmese, but these alert, docile pythons are simply nice pythons.

Indian Python
(*Python m. molurus*)

Although the Indian python (also called the Indian rock python) is the nominate form of *Python molurus*, it is a protected form (Appendix I, CITES) and as a result is not a common pet trade python. This sort of legal designation means that Indian pythons cannot be taken over state lines for commercial purposes without special permitation, but they can be sold commercially within that state with no restrictions. Most dealers avoid pythons that require special paperwork, especially for the larger kinds that have a limited market as well.

Appearance: Lighter in overall coloration than the Burmese, the Indian python also lacks the Burmese-definitive spearhead on top of the head.

Size: Adult at smaller sizes than the Burmese, the Indian is sexually mature at 8 to 12 feet (2.4–3.6 m). Some examples may reach 15 feet (4.6 m) or more.

Range: India, West Pakistan to Nepal, Sri Lanka.

Habitat: Like the Burmese, the Indian python can be found in open fields and in forested areas. It likes to live near permanent bodies of water, and is adept at swimming and climbing.

Breeding: Mating occurs in November through March. Clutch size is usually smaller than the Burmese, but more than 40 eggs have been reported. Egg deposition occurs from February to early June, with hatching from April to early August. Incubation follows the standard procedure on page 52.

Care Notes: Because this is a federally endangered species interstate or international sale or exchange requires permitation. However, if the Indian python has been intergraded with the Burmese or the Ceylon race at some time in the past, no permitation is required.

The disposition of the Indian python varies by individual and circumstances; some are, initially at least, impressively irascible. Most quiet with repeated gentle handling.

This ball python (Python regius) *has assumed the typical passive defensive pose. (See also photos on pages 12 and 49.)*

Ceylon Python
(*Python m. pimbura*)

This is a moderately sized python, reaching a length of 10 to 11 feet (3–3.4 m). It is found only on the island of Sri Lanka (formerly Ceylon). In appearance it resembles the Indian python most closely, but is perhaps little more intensely colored. It does not come under the regulations that encumber the Indian python, which makes it very attractive to hobbyists and dealers, for obvious reasons.

Ball Python
(*Python regius*)

The ball python is named for its habit of coiling in a tight ball when frightened, with its head in the center and protected by the body coils. As it becomes more accustomed to captivity, this behavior lessens and finally disappears. Its shyness/good disposition and ready availability in the wild have made it a very popular pet store snake, with some 40,000 being imported from Africa in 1994 alone. But not all of these snakes are imported as adults; in fact, these are mostly imported as hatchlings.

In Africa the snake hunters seek out the gravid female ball pythons. These are sold to the animal dealer, who holds the females until they deposit their eggs. Then the females are shipped out to the pet market, and the eggs held until the babies hatch. Those babies are then shipped out, to appear a few weeks later on the lists of wholesalers in the United States.

Appearance: The normal coloration of the ball python is a pretty combination of warm tan blotches over a black ground color. The head is distinct from the neck, even though this is a heavy-bodied snake. Labial pits are present, and are most evident toward the tip of the nose.

The enormous popularity of the ball python have made captive breeding for odd colors very profitable. In addition to the normal phase, golden, xanthic (lacking yellow) striped, and albino phases are being bred. Although another morph, the piebald phase, has been sporadically available in the past, the price that these snakes have commanded has placed them far out of the reach of most hobbyists. The value placed on piebald ball pythons has also made this morph a high priority in breeding programs, which is amazing when you consider that we are uncertain about the cause of the piebald coloration. Some believe the color to be a temperature-derived variant. We feel that because of the regular appearance of the piebald patterns in ball pythons, replicable genetics are involved. Piebalds have a normally colored head and tail between which are either one or two broad patches of patternless white coloration. If two, the coloration between the white sections is considered normal. Where visible, the normal coloration has a striped pattern. This is unusual in itself, but when seen in combination with the starkness of the white sections, the result is startlingly beautiful. All pattern and color changes are abruptly delineated.

Size: Hatchlings are about 9 inches (21 cm) long; adults range from about 3½ feet to 6 feet (.91–1.8 m).

Range: Western Africa.

Habitat: This basically terrestrial snake is found in western tropical Africa. It lives in scrub and semiaridland areas. It is a hunter, following rodent and other small animal prey far back into their burrows. Although not a tree-dwelling snake, it can climb quite well.

Breeding: Ball pythons can be sexed by comparing the size of the spurs; males generally have longer spurs. Probing is a more effective way to determine sex; males will probe to six subcaudal scales, the females to three.

Once you have a pair, a trio or even two pair, separate the sexes and use the standard cycling approach described on page 41 to ready them for breeding. During the cooling period, reduce the humidity in the cage by replacing the water bowl with one smaller. Maintain a daytime temperature of 76 to 80°F (25–27°C) and a nighttime low of 68 to 70°F (19–21°C).

At the end of the cooling period, begin to elevate the temperatures to their normal summer levels and place the sexes together. If you have a second male, he can be added temporarily to stimulate breeding activity. After the territorial defense behavior, remove the second male. Copulation should take place. If you have two pairs, the first male can be used reciprocatively to initiate breeding activity with the second pair.

If the snakes do not breed, separate them and try again in a week. Sometimes several introductions are necessary before breeding takes place.

Ovulation occurs in mid-March through April. Gravid females darken in color, a process thought to increase the body temperature when thermoregulating by basking. Gravid females may also bask with the posterior portion of the body turned upside down, under the cage's hot spot.

In the wild, ball pythons may deposit their eggs in the moist, humid area of mammal burrows. In captivity, they will enter an egg deposition box and deposit small clutches of large eggs.

Incubation takes about two months at a temperature of 87 to 90°F (31–32°C), and humidity needs to be about 90 to 95 percent.

If you choose maternal incubation, maintain cage temperatures at 85 to 89°F (29–32°C). Watch the female; if she uncoils from her eggs and leaves them, transfer them to your own incubator and take over the incubation process.

Care Notes: This python has been sold as the ultimate pet snake due to its gentle disposition, attractive appearance, and modest adult size.

The downside of ball python ownership is the snake's sporadic feeding. Ball pythons are famous—and rightly so, for this characteristic. They tend to prey imprint, and if your ball python fed on a particular type of wild rodent while still in Africa, you'd be hard-pressed to find an acceptable substitute. Like a two-year-old child who will eat only hot dogs, a ball python can demonstrate extraordinary resistance to any effort on your part to change its mind. Eight or nine months without eating doesn't seem to harm a ball python at all but it drives the owner slightly crazy!

Your ball python may not like laboratory mice, but may like black gerbils, or brown gerbils, or adult rats, or rat pups, guinea pigs of any of a half-dozen colors and coats, white-footed mice (we live-trapped a half-dozen and began

raising them ourselves), or particular color or variety of hamster. Try the prey items in different colors and both dead and alive. Sometimes exposing the brain of the prey item and leaving it in the doorway of the hide box will tempt your ball python to feed.

The Institute for Herpetological Research has found that a hide box made from an inverted clay flowerpot will sometimes provide a secure enough hiding spot to induce a ball python to feed. They enlarged the drain hole (using pliers to nip out the edges of the drain hole until the hole was large enough), and placed the flowerpot upside down in the cage. The ball python would rest inside the flowerpot, and peer over the edge to watch its potential prey item. IHR found the combination of this secure hiding area and offering live mice as food was one way to break the ball python's self-imposed fast. If you do try this technique, do not leave the mouse in the cage overnight; your mouse could decide to crawl inside the hide box to sample the snake within.

Reticulated Python (*Python reticulatus*)

The reticulated python is the classic python: big, beautiful, and sometimes uncannily predaceous. Some examples seem intent on driving their keeper away from the cage with alert, aggressive behavior that seems individually focused. By the same token, reticulateds that are habituated to their keeper(s) and to cage routines can pick up on any newcomers to the routine. Such ability to distinguish between humans is rather unusual in snakes and is of particular interest when the snake is as big (and potentially dangerous) as a reticulated python.

Appearance: The patterns of these snakes has been likened to an oriental rug in terms of variations on a theme of gold, olive, tan, brown, and dark

The reticulated python (Python reticulatus) *is the longest of the pythons. It displays a sporadically hostile demeanor and is not a good choice for a pet.*

gray blotches. The blotches are out-lined in black, against a silver gray body. Reticulated pythons also have the ability to change the shades and intensity of these colors. Eye color can range from orange-brown, to gray, to gray-green. Eye color and some dorsal patterns can be used to help identify retics from specific populations.

A beautiful snake that can lay 60 viable eggs per clutch and that is easy to breed in captivity will be bred especially for color morphs. Piebald and albino retics are part of current breeding programs. The albinos are a very showy pink, gold, and white.

Size: The retic is probably the largest of the pythons, topping out at over 30 feet (9 m). Most adults are smaller, from 10 to 16 feet (3.2–5.1 m) in length, and some isolated populations seem to average 8 feet (2.4 m). Hatchlings of the larger forms may be 24 inches (61 cm).

This is a slender species, much narrower in girth than a Burmese or rock python. Larger examples tend to put on weight as the growth rate slows; a 15-foot (4.6 m) retic will weigh 65 to 90 pounds (29–41 kg).

Origin: This widespread tropical python is known from Indonesia, Southeast Asia, the Philippines, and other Indo-Pacific islands.

Range/Habitat: In the wild, reticulated pythons like to be near water. They are good swimmers, swimming like other snakes with their head well out of the water and undulating from side to side for locomotion. Retics are also climbing snakes, finding both food and safety in trees overhead.

Breeding: Reticulated python males may get along during most of the year, but will certainly become combative as breeding season approaches. Combat generally includes slashing bites that may need suturing. These snakes breed in late summer/early fall, with eggs laid in early to mid-winter. The young emerge in 86 to 95 days when incubated at 88 to 91°F (31–33°C). If the female is allowed to maternally incubate her eggs, incubation is about 100 days.

Reticulated pythons produce large quantities of large eggs, up to 66 per clutch. The young feed readily and growth is rapid. Within the first year a once-baby reticulated can measure 10 feet (3.2 m) in length.

Care Notes: The beauty of reticulated pythons would seem to make them favorites in any python breeding program, but in truth these tend to be very big, very short-tempered, snakes. Reticulated pythons are known for their biting ability; the largest teeth in the front of the mouth are teardrop-shaped in cross section, with the sharp edge to the back. Specimens over 10 feet (3 m) in length, despite their narrow girth, should not be handled by a single individual.

The snakes feed readily; rabbits are the most easily obtained food item. Retics climb well and prefer to perch on elevated shelves and big branches in their cages. They also like to soak in their water container.

The African Rock Python (*Python sebae* ssp.)

The two subspecies of the African rock python are differentiated by distribution (*P. s. sebae* is found in central Africa, *P. s. natalensis* in southern Africa), adult size, and color. They are alike in their irascible nature.

African Rock Python, nominate form
Python sebae sebae

Appearance: The African rock python is beautifully patterned in gold and brown blotches that often join into a broad, irregular stripe. An undereye or subocular marking in the shape of a triangle is easily seen. Heat-sensory pits are on the upper and lower

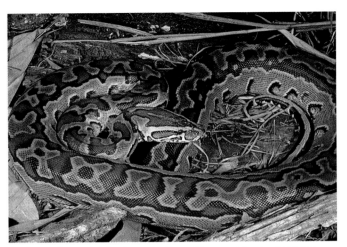

Its large size and (often) unruly disposition combine to make the African rock python (Python s. sebae) *a poor choice for most hobbyists.*

The Barkers found that males stop feeding in November, and male-to-male combat during the breeding season takes the form of wrestling more than the usual lunging and biting seen in other pythons. Females were not offered food after November, and both sexes were placed under the normal wintertime reduction of photoperiod. Nighttime temperatures during this period were 79 to 80°F (26–27°C), and daytime temps were 85 to 86°F (29–30°C). The females used their basking areas extensively as spring approached.

The sexes were introduced to each other in late December, with copulation taking place through February. The females ovulated in February; eggs were laid 54 days after ovulation.

Egg clutch size averaged 50 eggs, and the fertile eggs hatched after 79 days of incubation at 90°F (32.2°C). Neither female demonstrated thermoregulatory shivering when coiled around her eggs; the eggs were removed and placed inside an incubator.

Care Notes: These snakes do well if offered the same conditions as the reticulated or Burmese pythons. They need a large cage and at least a bathtub-sized water/soaking pool, but adjust well to captive foods. Most rock pythons are imports and do not alter their disposition as they mature. A few, acquired as hatchlings, may stay tame, but their potential size may tend to discourage friendly overtures on the part of their keeper.

The Barkers have noticed an unusual technique used by the African rock python when capturing prey, one previously unreported in other python species. The African rock python lunges past its prey, catching the prey in a fold of its neck. The snake turns, further coiling around its prey, and constriction actually begins before the item is seized in the snake's jaws.

labials. These snakes may fast for long periods of time (2½ years in captivity), but current thinking seems to be equating limited food intake with longevity.

Size: Adult at 8 to 12 feet (2.4–3.65 m), but can reach lengths in excess of 25 feet (7.6 m). Neonates are 18 to 23 inches (46–58 cm) upon hatching, and grow very fast.

Origin: Suitable habitat in a broad band across central Africa.

Range/Habitat: Adults are good swimmers and are found near water. Juveniles seem to be more terrestrial, and can be found in rocky areas and dry brushland.

Breeding: There's not much of a market for big, mean pythons like this, even if they are pretty. Snakes like the African rock python (both subspecies) may be placed in captive breeding programs in zoos or other institutions, but few people are serious about propagating these snakes. Dave and Tracy Barker are among those unusual few, and have worked with and bred African rocks.

Dwarf African rock python
(*Python sebae natalensis*)

In this case, the common name "dwarf" merely differentiates this 8- to 10-foot-long (2.4–3 m) race from the even larger nominate form.

Appearance: This variety can be distinguished from its larger cousin by several characteristics. Its overall coloration is darker; its dorsal markings tend to be well separated blotches rather than an irregular vertebral stripe. Its chin is dark and the subocular marking, which is characteristic of the larger form, is small or lacking.

Size: Adult at 8 to 14.5 feet (2.4–4.4 m). Young are about 14 inches (35.6 cm) at hatching.

Origin: This python is found in the southern third of the African continent.

Range/Habitat: Adults are found near permanent sources of water, both as a food source and for safety. Hatchlings are found in drier, rocky areas.

Breeding: Breeding techniques are the same as for the nominate form. Clutch size varies from 12 to 22 eggs.

Timor Python
(*Python timorensis*)

Timor pythons are rarely available in the pet market. They remain one of the most difficult pythons to breed in captivity.

Appearance: Although the overall color may vary, the pattern of the Timor python is rather standard. These pythons are most heavily patterned anteriorly and may be unicolored posteriorly. The ground color can vary from straw or olive to a rather bright yellow, and may be more brilliant by day than at night. The color of the pattern is a dark brown. Anteriorly, the snake may appeared barred, but this fragments and is difficult to describe by mid-body.

Range/Habitat: Timor pythons reputedly occur in open grasslands and open tropical forests of the islands of Timor and Flores, Indonesia.

Size: Timor pythons are a small, rather slender species. They are adult at some 6 feet (1.8 m) in total length.

Breeding: In truth, there have been few Timor pythons available to zoos and hobbyists in the United States. It is not surprising, therefore, that the species has been bred only a few times in captivity. The Dallas Zoo was the first to succeed; its success was echoed by Don Hamper, a talented breeder of many uncommon boa and python species. The eggs are large and the clutches small. An average of eight eggs are laid. April and June were the deposition months and at 90°F (33°C), incubation took 64 days. Although this is probably entirely coincidental, Hamper's breeders were both more than 15 years of age. Hatchlings are reportedly about 16 inches (41 cm) in total length.

Care Notes: These are not difficult snakes to keep, but they have proven difficult to cycle reproductively. It is fortunate that they are small, for they usually have rather feisty personalities and do not hesitate to strike far and accurately if bothered. Most secrete urates and feces when handled.

Their high cost (often upwards of $1,000) rather assures that only the most dedicated of hobbyists will be working with Timor pythons in the foreseeable future.

The Timor python (Python timorensis) *is a rare, expensive, and often irascible snake of moderate length.*

Useful Addresses and Literature

Despite the fact that many people keep and breed pythons, there are no "pythons only" clubs or societies. However, among the members of most herpetological societies are usually one or two individuals with a serious interest in these snakes.

To find your local herpetological society, ask biology teachers or professors, museum curators, the naturalists at your area nature center, or the staff at pet stores.

Amateur Herpetological Societies

Northern Ohio Association of Herpetologists (NOAH)
Department of Biology
Case Western Reserve University
Cleveland, OH 44106

Chicago Herpetological Society
2001 North Clark Street
Chicago, IL 60614

Gainesville Herpetological Society
P.O. Box 140353
Gainesville, FL 32614-0353

Central Florida Herpetological Society
P.O. Box 3277
Winter Haven, FL 33881

Northern California Herpetological Society
Box 1363
Davis, CA 95617-1363

Professional Herpetological Societies

Herpetologist's League
c/o Texas Natural Heritage Program
Texas Parks and Wildlife Department
4200 Smith School Road
Austin, TX 78744

Society for the Study of Amphibians and Reptiles
Department of Zoology
Miami University
Oxford, OH 45056

Magazines

Reptiles Magazine
P.O. Box 6050
Mission Viejo, CA 92690

Reptile and Amphibian Magazine
RD 3, Box 3709-A
Pottsville, PA 17901

Reptilian Magazine
22 Firs Close
Hazlemere, High Wycombe
Bucks HP15 7TF, England

Reptile Hobbyist Magazine
Third and Union Avenues
Neptune City, NJ 07753

Glossary

Albino Organism lacking pigment.

Ambient temperature Temperature of the surrounding environment.

Anterior Toward the front.

Anus External opening of the cloaca; the vent.

Arboreal Tree-dwelling.

Boid/Boidae Boas and pythons.

Brille Transparent "spectacle" covering the eyes of a snake.

Caudal Pertaining to the tail.

cb/cb Captive-bred, captive-born.

cb/ch Captive-bred, captive-hatched.

Cloaca Common chamber into which digestive, urinary, and reproductive systems empty, and that itself opens exteriorly through the vent or anus.

Constrict To wrap tightly in coils and squeeze.

Crepuscular Referring to dusk and/or dawn.

Deposition As used here, the laying of the eggs or birthing of young.

Deposition site Spot chosen by the female to lay her eggs or have young.

Dimorphic Difference in form, build, or coloration involving the same species; often sex-linked.

Diurnal Pertaining to daytime; pertaining to animals that are active in the daytime.

Dorsal Pertaining to the back; upper surface.

Dorsolateral Pertaining to the upper sides.

Dorsum Upper surface.

Ecdysis Shedding of the epidermis.

Ecological niche Precise habitat utilized by a species.

Ectothermic Cold-blooded.

Endothermic Warm-blooded.

Form: Identifiable species or subspecies.

Fossorial Adapted for burrowing; a burrowing species.

Genus Group of species having similar characteristics, the taxonomic designation that falls beneath family and above species. Genera, the singular of genus, is always capitalized.

Glottis The opening of the windpipe.

Gravid Reptilian equivalent of mammalian pregnancy.

Gular Pertaining to the throat.

Heliothermic Pertaining to a species that basks in the sun to thermoregulate.

Hemipenes Copulatory organs of male lizards and snakes. Singular: Hemipenis.

Herpetoculture Captive breeding of reptiles and amphibians.

Herpetology Study (often scientifically oriented) of reptiles and amphibians.

Hibernacula Winter dens.

Hybrid Offspring resulting from the breeding of two species.

Hydrate To restore body moisture by drinking or absorption.

Insular As used here, island-dwelling.

Intergrade To breed two subspecies.

Jacobson's organs Highly enervated olfactory pits in the palate of snakes and lizards.

Juvenile Young or immature.

Keel Ridge (along the center of a scale).

Labial Pertaining to the lips.

Lateral Pertaining to the side.

Loxoceminae Subfamily into which the New World burrowing python, *Loxocemus bicolor*, is often placed.

Melanism Profusion of black pigment.

Mental Scale at the tip of the lower lip.

Middorsal Pertaining to the middle of the back.

Midventral Pertaining to the center of the belly or abdomen.

Monotypic Containing but one type.

Nocturnal Active at night.

Ontogenetic Age-related (color) changes.

Oviparous Reproducing by means of eggs that hatch after laying.

Ovoviviparous Reproducing by means of shelled or membrane-contained eggs that hatch prior to, or at deposition.

Photoperiod Daily/seasonally variable length of the hours of daylight.

Pipping Opening the egg by means of an egg tooth, preparatory to hatching.

Poikilothermic Describing a species with no internal body temperature regulation; formerly termed cold-blooded.

Postocular To the rear of the eye.

Prehensile Adapted for grasping.

Prey imprinting Preferring prey only of a particular species and/or color.

Pythoninae Subfamily of the Boidae to which most pythons belong.

Race Subspecies.

Rostral Scale (often modified) on the tip of the snout.

Rugose Not smooth; wrinkled or tuberculate.

Saxicolous Rock-dwelling.

Scute Scale.

Species Group of similar creatures that produce viable young when bred; the taxonomic designation that falls beneath genus and above subspecies. Abbreviation: sp.

Subspecies Subdivision of a species; a race that may differ slightly in color, size, scalation, or other criteria. Abbreviation: ssp.

Sympatric Occurring together.

Taxonomy Science of classification of plants and animals.

Terrestrial Land-dwelling.

Thermoreceptive Sensitive to heat.

Thermoregulate To regulate (body) temperature by choosing a warmer or cooler environment.

Thigmothermic Pertaining to a species (often nocturnal) that thermoregulates by being in contact with a preheated surface such as a boulder or tarred road surface.

Vent External opening of the cloaca; the anus.

Venter Underside of a creature; the belly.

Ventral Pertaining to the undersurface or belly.

Ventrolateral Pertaining to the sides of the venter (belly).

Index

Pythons grow to sizes ranging from 2 to 20 feet (0.6 to 6.5 m) or longer. For this reason, it is important that you understand the ramifications of python ownership, particularly if you have chosen a giant species. This hatchling green tree python, *Morelia viridis*, yellow at birth, will turn green as it matures. It will probably reach 6 feet (1.8 m) in length as an adult.